HONOLKA COURAGE

SHARON HONOLKA

authorHOUSE

AuthorHouse™
1663 Liberty Drive
Bloomington, IN 47403
www.authorhouse.com
Phone: 833-262-8899

This book is a work of non-fiction. Unless otherwise noted, the author and the publisher make no explicit guarantees as to the accuracy of the information contained in this book and in some cases, names of people and places have been altered to protect their privacy.

Published by AuthorHouse 04/27/2021

ISBN: 978-1-6655-2219-9 (sc)
ISBN: 978-1-6655-2238-0 (e)

Library of Congress Control Number: 2021907303

Print information available on the last page.

This book is printed on acid-free paper.

CONTENTS

DEDICATION AND ACKNOWLEDGEMENT

June 2019, Eva Honolka Newman asked "Honolka Courage" be dedicated to the tens of thousands of refugees that had the courage to flee his or her country because of political persecution, war, or violence.

Eva gratefully acknowledged the United States of America who kindly adopted the Honolka Family. Offering freedom of race, religion, nationality, or political opinion.

Thanking her parents, Jarmila and John Honolka, Sr., for the courage to pursue their dreams for the benefit of their five children. Teaching them to remain strong during the difficult times

ABOUT ME AND THE HONOLKA STORY

According to the Merriam Webster Dictionary, a writer is 'one who expresses ideas in writing' or 'one engaged in literary work. 'An author is 'a person who writes a novel, poem, essay etc., the composer of a literary work. 'I do not consider myself an author or writer. I do not even enjoy reading for pleasure. If you find errors in grammar or punctuation, please note I, Sharon Honolka, am also not an English major.

What I am is Eva's Honolka Newman's sister-in-law that was asked to put "her stuff" in some type of order. This process started May of 2019. As of February 2, 2021, I have fulfilled my promise to Eva Honolka Newman and retained Author House for publication.

Materials have been gathered from various sources. You will read duplications, especially when you start reading her speeches as they appeared in local newspapers. Eva was a remarkable patriotic public speaker that love the United States of America and respected The American Flag.

Recently I was asked by a relative, "who are you getting to edit the book"? Curious to the response, I asked, "what does an editor do"? It was quiet. Then they said, "well, they take out what they don't think should be there, or re-word a sentence". My response was, "I don't want anything removed or re-worded". What people will be reading was handwritten by family matriarch, Eva Honolka Newman, her brothers, sister, children, grandchildren, nieces, and nephews. Numerous newspaper articles were re-typed, word for word, giving credit to the source and writer. This book is a nonfiction narrative writing based on personal memories.

By the time you finish reading, you will have walked in the shoes of John and Jarmila Honolka and their five children. You will have retraced the steps taken by the seven Honolka's through the trials, tribulation, distress, frustration, and suffering of a family seeking freedom.

Endless hours, days, weeks, and months have been spent gathering articles, asking questions, documenting responses, and verifying facts. I thank my husband, Don Honolka for his time and patience. Often taking him back to many unpleasant memories.

Without the positive support of Don, and the guidance of my "Heavenly Father" telling me "You Can Do This," this task would not have been completed. Don also told me, "You are going to have to have thick skin because you will be criticized and people will remember events differently". Fortunately, I am just repeating Eva's words.

As always. the Lord has been by my side. I thank Him. To Him I give the glory, praise, and honor.

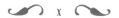

WHAT YOU WILL LOVE

MEMORIES FROM THE FAMILY OF John and Jarmila Honolka during 1937 – 2020. You will follow their life in a one-of-a-kind accounting during wartime Czechoslovakia. Surviving and moving from the Nazi's and the Russian's. Only to arrive in the United States of America and continuing through challenging times.

Letters written in German to John's Mother, Bertha, have been translated. He wrote often and was careful not to share alarming news so she would worry.

It is hard to imagine saying good-bye to your parents at the age of 43 and 32 knowing there was a strong possibility that you would never see them again, or in Jarmila's case, not being allowed to visit her homeland. In addition to explaining to your young family of five what is happening in their life.

Only our "Heavenly Father" knew how this journey would impact the future of their eldest child, Eva Honolka. Her gift of mentoring others by sharing her life story.

The following pages are based on facts, real events, and real people. Parts are self-written by Eva Honolka Newman that are a collection of her memories, often given in public speaking forums.

You will have the opportunity to read numerous newspaper articles. Many published about Eva as a cherished mentor to the Maxwell-Gunter Air Force Base, which is a United States Air Force installation

under the Air Education and Training Command. It was easy for Eva to related to these young Czech pilots, being the wife of deceased LTC Frank Charles Newman.

The memories of John and Jarmila's grandchildren were documented and presented to their parents on Thanksgiving 2012. You do not realize what a child remembers from the past. What is important and what was not so important to the child.

You know a mother means a lot when you email "The Ladies Home Journal" about her life. You will read the submission made by Eva's daughter Julie Newman Slaten.

Read Eva's favorite scriptures. She always had a strong faith and often wondered why she was put through over 80 years of continuous trials, heartaches, difficulties, and hardships. She would shrug her shoulders, shake her head, look at you with those bright baby blue eyes and say, "Maybe my story will give comfort, peace or ease the pain of another.".

WHO'S WHO

John Honolka, Sr.

HANS (AKA JAN, JON, AND John) Honolka was born on December 29, 1909, in Litomerice, Czechoslovakia, his father, Josef was 41 and his mother, Berta Maria, was 20. He had three sons and two daughters with Jarmila Kralik between 1937 and 1950. He died on April 26, 1983, in Arlington TX, at the age of 73.

John Honolka was an accomplished athlete. He played soccer on the national Team called Sparta Slavia and in the winter season hockey. He also was a skier and won a medal against Sweden ski jumping.

After he married, Jarmila Kralik, he concentrated on his business and sports; those were his passions. His physical strength, awesome timing and speed made him extraordinarily strong. He had the capability of thinking outside the box. Looking at the grey not just black and white. A true visionary. A master at quick important decision making. He was ahead of his time in ideas and planning.

He built three villas in Trutnov, Czechoslovakia: one for his family and two others for some of his co-workers. The house that the Honolka's lived in had two apartments. John, Sr., and family lived upstairs, and his parents lived downstairs. In that era elderly parents lived with their children.

Patricia, the youngest daughter, recalls they were the only home in the city of Trutnov to have their cellar turned into a garage.

Don remembers John Honolka, Sr.

I remember my father most for his good business ethics. Sometimes my father placed more emphasis on business than family. Only to take care of his family. Father was always one step ahead of everything.

I believe my father was stern for my benefit. His challenges would encourage me to achieve my goals (or his goals) and in the end I felt like a winner. His standard goals were larger than the average man.

My father was a "work when you work" and "play when you play" type of person.

From my father, I learned the importance of being honest, being a perfectionist and having good mannerisms.

He often said: "Don't take no SXXX off of anybody". "Stand your ground if your right."

My father's favorite quotes were:

"An aggressive man will work today and play tomorrow."

"A lazy man will play today and work tomorrow."

"Twelve-hour day is only a half a day's work."

"America is the land of opportunity."

Every man has a hero, I am fortunate, because I have two – MY PARENTS

> Don wrote this in 1992, at the age of 53.

From family, Sharon learned early in her relationship with Don that he is much like his father. Very direct speaking, goal oriented, business focused, prefers a routine, hard worker, enjoys privacy and can be very

loyal. He speaks firmly and will tell you exactly what he thinks if you like it or not.

One habit he picked up from his father is to always dress appropriately and wear well buffed polished shoes. We use shoe trees and shoes are hand polished weekly.

Jarmila Kralik Honolka

When Jarmila Kralik was born on July 6, 1920, in Trutnov, Czechoslovakia, her father Rudolph Kralik, was 41 and her mother, Marie (Roubicek) was 39. She died on August 26, 1987, in Arlington, TX, at the age of 67, it is said, "due to a broken heart." PC found Jarmila lying on her bathroom floor from heart failure. This happened just a few weeks after the Czech Embassy refused to allow her to attend her brother's (Olda) memorial service in the Czech Republic. They would only allow her to go if she denounced her Czech citizenship. Which she would not consider.

Jarmila was an exceptionally talented woman. Her many crafts included, needle point, crocheting, drawing, painting, cooking, and sewing. In earlier years Jarmila sewed gold into the hem line of the girl's dresses to be used later during travel.

Don recalls days in the Amana Colonies that his friends always ended up at the Honolka home around time to eat. Jarmila enjoyed cooking and watching people eat.

While visiting Angie Honolka, Tom's daughter, in January 2017 she shared many stories of her mother, Janeen, being taught to cook by Jarmila. Even pulling out the recipe file to find a handwritten recipe by Jarmila for Sauerkraut Soup.

All Jarmila's children have inherited towels, napkins, tablecloths, dresser scarfs, and ornaments of her craft. Her children cherish these items. Many have been kept to donate to the National Czech & Slovak Museum & Library in Cedar Rapids, IA.

Don and I have spent hours at the Czech Museum. It is our goal to have a section in the library detail the journey of the Honolka family to the United States of America. The section would be educational of a historic period. It is our dream that someday future Czech generations will show some interest in our history.

Eva Honolka Newman

Eva Honolka was born on May 14, 1937, in Trutnov, Czechoslovakia. Her father, Hans, was 27, and her mother, Jarmila, was 16. Prior to 1939 the family moved to Nova Paka. Eva remembered living close to a military base. Later in life she realized the impact that military base would have on her life.

Eva Wrote this in the Spring of 2019

How strange that after eighty-two years of my life, I feel the urge to share the journey that was my Kaleidoscope of experiences, or as I say, "my lot in life.'

By God's grace I have risen above the trepidation, the pain of separation from one's homeland, the loss of identity when caught up in the upheavals of governments wanting to own your heart and soul, that chain you to the yoke of mental slavery.

My lot in life was to "accept the things I could not change," realizing that I came with nothing into this world, and that I would leave not taking anything with me, but with God's blessings I would come to the end of my journey with total victory.

Everything in between, family, children, personal possessions, will be a gift from God, loaned to me for my life. Under all circumstances I thank my Heavenly Father for all that He gives me. Good or bad, for "Greater is He who is in me, than he who is in the world."

I write these pages with great affection for this nation called America, that so generously adopted me and took our family out of the mire and despair, with the promise to pursue happiness and hope. We realized that we must bring happiness to life ourselves, and with the undergirding of God, we will be successful.

I have always felt that it is a must to pay back to this Nation that so graciously adopted us, and our Heavenly Father who guided us.

With great purpose, we studied the Constitution and the Bill of Rights. We were law abiding citizens. We learned the English language and understood the great privilege of voting.

"Give me liberty or give me death." The words of Patrick Henry became our motto, and yes, we joined the military to protect the precious liberty and this way of life. We became God fearing, law abiding United States of America citizens.

In an enchanting mountain region called Krkonose, also known as the Sudetenland, by the German population is a small town called Trutnov, Czechoslovakia. Czechoslovakia is now known as the Czech Republic and has been so known since the Velvet Revolution of 1989.

I was born May 14, 1937, at five minutes to eight on a Friday morning. My Mother was just sixteen years old, my Father twenty-six. My Father was a professional soccer (football) player on the Czech national team, Sparta Slavia. My Father was also an exceptionally good businessman and was active in the food industry.

My parent's apartment was next to a military training facility in Trutnov. Such installations are known in many European nations as a Kasarna.

Our apartment windows faced a large meadow, and by my Mother's description, the meadow was a full of bloom with yellow dandelions (Pampelisky), and small white daisies.

A midwife delivered me, and I weighed four pounds, and was nineteen inches in length.

The air smelled of early Spring, and the sunlight glided the mountain tops with pure touches of gold.

My Mother, Jarmila, read a novel before I was born about an adventurous young woman whose life took her on many journeys to many countries. The character Eva captivated my mother's imagination and she made up her mind that if the baby were a girl, she would be named Eva.

And so, my life began in May 1937. There was an uncomfortable feeling, the chill of political upheaval was on the horizon.

Hitler had set his vision on Czechoslovakia, and the mountains of Krkonose, where a certain number of German people lived, and had for some time lived in harmony with the Czechs.

Don Honolka

Vladimir, also known as Don and Lada, was born June 21, 1939, in Nova Paka, Czechoslovakia. Eva was 2 years old. As the eldest two of five children they have more distinct memories prior to arriving in the United States of America. Memories that have affected them and their children. Don remembers attending school in four different countries.

As Don's wife. I did not have the opportunity to meet John and Jarmila Honolka. Although, I have listened to frequent stories over the past 32 years. Patricia told me Don inherited much of his behavioral style from his father. Don takes after John, Sr. being results-oriented, no excuses, direct, self-confident, driven, calculating, critical, athletic, honest and most of all an organized perfectionist. Don learned business from manufacturing, distribution, marketing, and sales of a product directly from his father. The total package.

At the age of 18 years old, Don remembering unloading 100-pound bags of flour at the bakery in Amana. Recruiting his friends to help for a good wage. His friends only helped once. It was hard work.

When it came time for his first car, he was told "You work all summer in the bakery and you will have your first car, plus money for insurance." At that time, in this family, cars where not bought for children. Honolka children had to earn the money and purchase their own automobiles.

Often Don would have to get up at 3AM to do a bakery route before attending school.

Recently Don and I were talking about what he sees happening in the United States during 2020. He said "I am glad my parents are not here to see certain elements of people talking like they support socialism as opposed to communism. Whenever government starts talking about free this and free that it is the beginning of communism. You will have a controlled society. You will be told what you must do and what you cannot do."

All his brothers and sisters have told me that John and Jarmila would have highly approved of our marriage. Don and I are very much alike and work well together as a team. We currently reside in Springtown, Texas.

Vlasta Patricia Honolka

Vlasta, known as Patricia in the United States, was born on July 7, 1942, in Nova Paka, Czechoslovakia, Eva was 5 years old. During the past thirty years they were like wine and cheese, peanut butter and jelly or salt and pepper. A day did not go by without a telephone conversation. Everything Eva knew Patricia knew, good, bad, and ugly. The most difficult year in Patricia's life was 2019 when personal medical issues took priority to being by Eva's side. Patricia chose a kind professional and retired after 39 years as a hospital RN. She currently resides in Kansas.

During November of 2020, Patricia sent a note which I feel is worth sharing word for word, "Mother was a small beautiful intelligent, gentle, kind soul who fought valiantly to keep her family alive. We may have been hungry, but we did not starve to death. We may have been cold, but we did not freeze to death. We were kept clean so we would not come down with any bugs or diseases. She would provide the best she could with what there was and there was not much. Occasionally we would receive a "Care" package from the United States delivered by the Red Cross.

One Spring I had outgrown all my shoes. Autumn came, frost was on the ground and still no shoes, not for a kid in a refugee camp. Mother found a piece of cardboard and stood me on it while she traced my feet, then cutout the tracing. Shoes were being made. They looked more like slippers, but I had shoes and my feet were warmer.

Vladimir (Don) had outgrown his brown corduroy jacket, mother cut the back out, split the fabric in half and placed cardboard cut outs in the center of each half. The corduroy and cardboard were sewn by hand with needle and thread. A flap was formed, a buttonhole was made and a button from the front of the jacket was used to close the flap.

I will always remember my mother's kindness, patience, and tolerance.

John "JJ" Honolka, Jr.

John Honolka Jr. was born on June 8, 1946, in Trutnov, Czechoslovakia, when Eva was 9 years old.

At the age of ten, "JJ enjoyed getting up early to ride with his brother Don on routes. Only because Don would let him drive the truck.

John enlisted in the Navy and became part of the recruit training class of December 26, 1963 at Great Lakes, Illinois.

Before John, Sr retired he expanded the Amana Bakery to Texas where John, Jr. was in charge. Also, following in his father's footsteps, "JJ" wanted to be independent. He chose the automobile industry.

It was in the automobile industry that he earned the name "JJ". You would assume using that nickname his middle name starts with a "J", it does not. John does not have a middle name. He said, "in the automobile industry no one could pronounce "Honolka" or remember the name "Honolka", so I came up with something catchy, "JJ". To this day he is called "JJ".

JJ was well known for smoking brisket, ribs and chicken. His were the best.

His widow, Sandra, currently resides in Justin, Texas.

Tom Honolka

The youngest Honolka is Tomas Jaromir Honolka born March 14, 1950, in Lindau, Germany, when Eva was 12 years old. The family was living in a displaced person camp for a year prior to Tom being born. Patricia recalls, he was delivered by Nuns in a convent. Tom was very frail and small due to the lack of Jarmila's nutrition.

Tom retired from the largest commercial baking product company in the United States as a remarkably successful Sales Market Manager. One year selling 5 million dollars' worth of product. His routes became so large the company had to split his routes. Tom continued to rebuild them only to be split once more. Once again following in his father's ways.

During November 2020, Patricia sent me the following note regarding Tom:

"Tom was a beautiful baby; however, he was fragile, mother took care of him like a baby bird. Food was scarce, anything good that could be cooked, pureed, mashed, or smashed was off limits to the rest of us, it was for the little bird. A carrot would be cooked and mashed. An apple was scraped with a spoon to make a sauce, there were no graters. An occasional cup of cream of wheat became available, that was priceless. Tom thrived and grew up to be a healthy, bright man. The last thirty years he has been involved with a service organization sponsoring members and being an inspirational speaker

If it were not for Tom and Leslie, Sharon and Don would have never met. We were all in the same place at the same time. I am not sure who approached whom first, regardless, we have been together since May 20, 1989.

Sharon's favorite quote of Tom's is "Keep the Faith."

Tom and Leslie currently reside in Nashville, Arkansas.

Oldrich Kralik

Oldrich Kralik was the son of Marie and Rudolph Kralik and Jarmila Honolka's brother. He had one brother, Milek and three sisters, Maria, Jarmila and Vlasta Zirovnicky. Currently place and dates are unknown for the Kralik children. Oldrich was in the Czech military and was planning to come to the United States of America with the Honolka family. The communistic government captured Oldrich and sent him from Hungry to Czechoslovakia to stand trial. He was sentenced to a life of hard labor. Later you will read a letter John Honolka sent to his parents, October 9, 1948 referencing Oldrich.

Philip Carroll Callahan

Philip Carroll Callahan "PC" was born March 5, 1943 and passed May 11, 2017, at the age of 74. He is buried in Montgomery, AL. He had a very disciplined childhood education and served as a Combat Marine in Vietnam. "PC" was placed in Eva's life during her employment in Montgomery, Alabama. He was a Sargent, appointed by Governor Wallace's to the Alabama White House police force.

Often PC would survey the Confederate White House where Eva was the Supervisor. The two of them became close friends. He was like a younger brother looking out for his big sister. Both having a great sense of humor, loved life and could spend hours talking about history.

With only one year prior to retirement, "PC" resigned from the State Capitol and moved to Arlington, TX to assist in the care of Eva's mother, Jarmila. After Jarmila's death in 1987, PC returned to Montgomery and was reinstated with full benefits at the State Capitol until his retirement.

At this time, he reunited with Nesta, his High School sweetheart. They married October 22, 2001. Remaining in Montgomery, Alabama.

"PC" enjoyed trains. During a February 2020 visit, Nesta showed Don and Sharon his "Train Room", just as he left it in May of 2017.

Arvis Dwain Williams

Arvis Dwain Williams was born December 28, 1933 in Oklahoma. Sharon met Eva and Arvis for the first time, September 3, 1989. The four of them hooked up in Vicksburg, Mississippi.

Sharon felt she was in a history class listening to Eva share the American Civil War history as they toured the Vicksburg National Military Park. Arvis documenting our journey through the lens of his camera.

Arvis has been traced back to Montgomery, Alabama as early as 1976. Stories are that he was a photojournalist for Maxwell Air Force Base and retired Air Force.

Arvis was an excellent photographer and writer. He stood by Eva's side for more than 30 years. Scheduling and accompanying her to speaking engagements, trips to the Czech Republic and acting as her managing publicist.

"PC" and Arvis contributed greatly to Eva's life and started the documentation of this book. She considered them much more than friends; they were family.

Tom and Patricia would write to Arvis. Sharon wrote to him after Eva's last stroke. Upon receipt of Sharon's letter, Arvis called. You could tell on the telephone he was extremely upset and sad. He wanted to speak with her, which was not possible

Arvis moved on to the other side March 14, 2020 – alone.

Frank Charles Newman
July 5, 1927 – February 24, 1970

Frantisek, (Frank) Charles Newman was born in Nepomuk, Czechoslovakia on July 5th, 1927. Newman's birthplace is one both revered and renowned in Czech history. "Frank" was educated in the schools of his hometown, and very soon distinguished himself as a profoundly serious scholar.

Frank Newman's record of scholarship and intellect led to his entering the renowned Charles University in Prague. Charles University, then as now, is one of the most renowned and respected institutions of higher learning in the world.

It was while in attendance at Charles University that Frank once more established a record of scholarship matched by few others. He studied Philosophy, Law and Languages. At one point began serious preparation for the Roman Catholic Priesthood.

By the time of the Nazi occupation, and the closure of Charles University by the German authorities, Frank had achieved both written and spoken proficiency in no less than six languages. Frank was held in the highest esteem by both faculty and fellow students.

With the re-opening of the university at the end of the war, and the re-establishment of Czech sovereignty, Frank became vitally interested in the politics of the time, and saw, as many students did, the coming of yet another repressive regime, this time in the form of Communism.

With the Communist "Putch" in 1948, Czechoslovakia once more came under the odious heel of an oppressor, this time a very much home grown one. Frank found himself, as did thousands, a displaced person. Persons, who though they longed for their former home, could no longer return to it, and live under tyranny and oppression.

It was while in the Displaced Person's Camp during 1949 in Lindau, Germany, that Frank Newman met and became friends with the family of John Honolka. This event would have signal significance in the years to come.

While still in displaced person status, Frank was afforded the opportunity to enlist in the United States Army, which he did in 1952. Frank served as an enlisted soldier until 1955, at which time he was offered the opportunity to attend Officer Candidate School.

This opportunity came about largely as the result of Corporal Frank Newman's assignment as an enlisted aide to Major General Bolling, the Theatre Commander. General Bolling recognized Frank's inherit soldierly qualities, his education, his deportment and bearing, and felt that the Army could be better served by Frank's attendance at Officer Candidate School.

Due to Frank's status as a non-United States citizen, waivers from the Army High Command would be required for Newman to attend Officer Candidate School. General Bolling placed his full weight behind the waiver, and Frank was ordered to Officer Candidate School.

Upon graduation from "OCS", Frank was commissioned a 2nd Lieutenant of Artillery in the United States Army. Thus, a new chapter in Frank's service to his adopted land was begun.

Lt Newman was ordered to Army flight training and awarded his wings in December of 1956. Flight status brought with it a long series of aviation duty assignments, and once more, Frank distinguished himself in the performance of his duty.

Frank Newman simply loved to fly, and if there is any such thing as a "born pilot", Frank certainly was one.

Franks duty assignments took him both to Korea and to Germany, a location somewhat closer to Frank's native Czechoslovakia. As Frank was advancing through the officer ranks, increasingly challenging and responsible assignments came his way. He handled his assignments with dedication and professionalism. Qualities once more noted by peers and superiors alike.

Frank qualified to fly helicopters in 1960. This fact was to have increasing significance as the Army's "Air Cavalry" concept was now rapidly taking shape. Frank found himself once more in Germany, this time assigned to the 14th Armored Cavalry Regiment.

Completing his tour with the 14th Cavalry, Frank was then assigned to the 11th Air Assault Division, stationed at Ft. Benning, Georgia. The 11th Air Assault Division became the 1st Cavalry Division, thus resurrecting one the Army's most famed combat formations.

Frank accomplished his command to Vietnam in August of 1965, as a part of the massive troop buildup in the former French Indochina. Here, Frank served his first combat tour. Upon returning to the United States, in July of 1966. Frank was then stationed at the Army Aviation Center, at Fort Rucker in Alabama. Frank was a flight instructor, and subsequently became Chief of the Foreign Military Training Division.

In March of 1968, still an Artillery Officer, was assigned to the Advanced Artillery School at Fort Sill, Oklahoma. Once more, Frank, excelled in the academic setting, and his scholarship and leadership were manifested to fellow student officers and instructors as well.

It is perhaps, at this point that I should relate to you how Frank Newman came into my life, and how he would shape it so profoundly. As I noted previously, my parents had met and became friends with Frank while we were all at the Displaced Persons Camp in Lindau, Germany. Currently, I was eleven years of age, and Frank was twenty-one.

Frank was working in the camp, and was well known for his competence, care, and compassion for others. Upon our immigration to the United States and Frank's enlistment in the Army, our paths diverged, but only as it turned out, for a while.

By now my family was living in South Amana, Iowa, where my Father ran the Amana Society Bakery. I had graduated from South Amana High School and had been awarded a scholarship to the Art Institute in Chicago, Illinois.

Throughout my teenage years, I had always dreamed of the "Prince Charming" with whom I would fall madly in love, and with whom I would sail off into the sunset. Such was not to be however, nor would I go to pursue my education as an artist.

My Father told me quite plainly that Chicago was no fit place for a young girl alone, and that quite simply, I would not go to Chicago. No, I would go instead, to Austin, Texas and that I would marry Frank Charles Newman, who by now was a Lieutenant in the U. S. Army. I was not happy in the least with this 'arranged' marriage, but I had been raised to honor my Father and my Mother.

So, instead of college in Chicago, I was bound for an arranged marriage in Austin, Texas. I would marry a man I really did not know, and anxiety and uncertainty were at the top of my range of emotions at the time. I now did what any young woman would do in a similar situation, I cried.

To my Mother I exclaimed, "I don't want to get married". Mother said to me, "Eva, if you marry out of love you have thin glasses on your eyes. You do not see reality. And sometime when you take them off, you do see reality. It is not all gold that glitters".

On July 4, 1956, I was on an airplane bound for Austin, Texas. I was married to Frank Charles Newman on July 7, 1956 in a Catholic ceremony, at the age of 19. When we went back to our apartment, I must tell you, "Rigor Mortis" set in.

It was at this point that I discovered what an honorable, kind, and sensitive man I had married. Frank made allowances for my fear, anxiety, and uncertainty. Our wedding night was considerably different than most. Frank suggested that I sleep in the bedroom, while he slept on the couch. We now began a period of "courtship".

For the next three months, though we were married, essentially, we dated. Frank taught me to bowl. We frequently went out to dinner, and saw many, many movies. It was at this time, and in the time-honored tradition of the soldier, that Frank received orders to Korea. While Frank was in Korea, I returned to the Amana, pregnant and lived with my parents.

Frank wrote to me each day that he was away, and you should know that his tour in Korea lasted eighteen months. I thought, and still do, that for Frank to write so faithfully, and in the manner that he did, was above and beyond the call of duty. I still have all those letters after all these years. They are numbered in the sequence that they were written, and that I received them.

Among those cherished letters is one of very significance. It was written during Frank's first combat tour in Vietnam. Frank's helicopter had crashed in Viet Cong territory, and they were actively searching for the crew of the downed aircraft. While hiding under the helicopter, Frank found a scrap of paper and wrote these words, "I am writing you today to let you know that under all conditions and circumstances, I love you and our children".

Luck, that often intangible and fickle soldier's luck was with Frank that day, and he was rescued. Frank's first act upon reaching safety was to write a regular letter in which he enclosed the note quoted above.

We had four children. Our first child, Michael Frank Newman, died during childbirth on April 6, 1957. He is buried in Marengo, Iowa. Our second child, Michael David Newman was born June 14, 1959, Flag Day, in Fort Devens, Massachusetts. Mike is currently living in Atlanta, Georgia. Our third child, Julie Ann was born in Beb Herfedal, Germany on July 9, 1961 and is currently living in Birmingham, Alabama. Our fourth, and final child, Steven Alan (Chip) Newman was born February 28, 1963 also in Beb Herfedal, Germany. Chip was killed by a drunk driver on Flag Day, June 14, 1980 in Vernon, Florida at the age of 17. Chip's date of death was also Mike's 21st birthday.

"For I shall go to the altar of God. To God, the joy of my youth".

During my life, I have spent much time on the speaking and lecture circuit. In this "Magnificent Obsession", I am motivated, not only by Frank Charles Newman's life and service to our nation, but by own desire to pay back, at least a little, to the nation which adopted us.

I am keenly aware that the Lord has a mission for my life, and that in a manner of speaking, it is a continuation of Frank's mission to service to his God, Honor, Duty and Country. While Frank's mortal duty on this earth is done, the mission nevertheless continues, until the point I am silenced.

LTC Frank Charles Newman's service to his adopted land, and to the land to which he gave so much, lasted some eighteen years. In this time frame, and as a member of the United States Army, Frank, rose from Private to the Grade of Lieutenant Colonel.

LTC Newman was not simply an aviator, he was a passionate aviator. He amassed some 3,500 flying hours and was proficient in some twenty-two types of both fixed wing and rotary aircraft. At the time of his death, LTC Newman held status as a "Master Aviator".

In many ways an unlikely soldier, Frank held numerous awards and decorations, which include the Distinguished Flying Cross, The Legion of Merit, The Bronze Star, Vietnamese Order of the Palm, twenty-two Air Medals, and numerous additional awards and commendations.

Frank Charles Newman has left a priceless legacy. He was a man of true humility, as most heroes are, he was a man of gentleness. He was sensitive, kind, and caring, an ideal husband and father. In addition to these attributes, Frank, was a man of unbending integrity, and uncompromising principles and ethics. He did not find it necessary to speak or lecture on these qualities, he lived them. He was too many, the ideal commanding officer. He asked nothing of others that he had not done or was not willing to do. He was honored and respected by his soldiers.

As the firing party rendered its final salute, one envisions the rider less horse, boots revered in the stirrups, saber slung from the saddle, led by the solemn soldier. The Warrior is borne to his final resting place, flag draped coffin on the artillery caisson. This vision is somewhat metaphorical, except for the firing party, the sounding of "Taps", and the "Missing Man Formation" flown by Frank Newman's fellow aviators from nearby Fort Rucker, Alabama.

LTC Frank Charles Newman now rest not far from Fort Rucker, a post made better for his having been there, an Army made better for having proudly served in it.

Ecclesiastes 3: 1-8 KJV

To everything there is a season,
and a time to every purpose under the heaven:
A time to be born, a time to die;
a time to plant, and a time to pluck up that which is planted;
A time to kill, and a time to heal;
a time to break down, and a time to build up;
A time to weep, and a time to laugh;
a time to mourn, and a time to dance;
A time to cast away stones, and a time to gather stones together;
a time to embrace, and a time to refrain from embracing;
A time to get, and a time to lose;
a time to keep, and a time to cast away;
A time to rend, and a time to sew;
a time to keep silence, and a time to speak;
A time to love, and a time to hate;
A time of war, and a time of peace.

Death came to LTC Frank Charles Newman out of the soft blue of a Vietnamese sky. It was his time, and those of us who honor his life, his service, his legacy, will always be tempted to ask "Why?'.

I will not attempt to answer that question, for to do so lies far beyond my power. Suffice it to say the Frank Charles Newman, LTC of Artillery, U.S. Army is one more immortal link in the "Long Blue Line" which dates to the very founding of the Republic. The Army is better for Frank simply having served in it. We are better people for simply having known Frank, for having loved him, experienced his love, for having served alongside and with him. Most of all for being inspired by his example of "God, Honor, Duty and Country".

LTC Frank Charles Newman is honored on Panel 13W, Line 51 Vietnam Veterans Memorial.

Legion of Merit Presented to Ozark Widow

Posthumous awards, including the Legion of Merit, earned by LTC Frank C. Newman were presented to his widow, Mrs. Eva Honolka Newman of Ozark. LTC Newman was killed in an aircraft accident in Vietnam on February 24, 1970.

In Making the presentation Major General Delk M. Oden, Commanding General at Ft. Rucker, and Commandant of the Army Aviation School, stated the LTC Newman, a native of Czechoslovakia, "was a man who appreciated life in this country for himself and his family."

The Legion of Merit, Distinguished Flying Cross, the Bronze Star Medal, Purple Heart and Air Medal with 19 Oak Leaf Clusters honored LTC Newman's service for the period October 1969 to February 1970 while he served in Vietnam as commanding officer, 131st Aviation Company, 212th Combat Aviation Battalion, 1st Aviation Brigade.

According to the citation accompanying the Legion of Merit, the nation's second highest award for outstanding achievement, he "consistently demonstrated efficient responsiveness to the myriad problems inherent in conducting operations in a hostile combat environment".

"Through the application of dynamic leadership, rare foresight, and sound principles of management, he was able to direct his company in attaining an exemplary record of mission accomplishment."

The citation further stated that "through his courage, initiative and fidelity LTC Newman earned the respect and admiration of all with whom he served and made a material contribution in the free world effort to thwart communist aggression in the Republic of Vietnam.

In addition to Mrs. Newman, the Colonel is survived by three children, Michael 11, Julie 8, and Steven 7. They accompanied their mother to the ceremony in MG Oden's office.

LTC Newman enlisted in the U. S. Army in Germany in 1952 and was stationed at Ft. Rucker as chief of the Foreign Military Training Division from 1966 until 1968.

Descendants for John and Jarmila Honolka

Eva Honolka Newman   DOB: 05/14/1937 DOD: 09/13/2020

 Michael Frank Newman DOB: 04/06/1957 DOD: 04/06/1957

 Michael David Newman

  Melanie Newman

  Stephanie Anne Newman Burris

   Baby Girl

 Julie Ann Newman Slaten

  Kelly Diane Slaten

  Brian Andrew Slaten

  Amy

 Steven Alan Newman   DOB: 02/28/1963 DOD: 06/14/1980

 Sidney Homer Honolka Walker DOB: 03/03/1974 DOD: 07/08/1977

 John Zeke Honolka Walker DOB: 11/10/1971 DOD: 11/13/1971

Don Honolka

 Jack Michael Honolka

 James (Jim) Donald Honolka

 Jon (Beatle) Jeffrey Honolka DOB: 03/18/1963 DOD: 05/16/2013

 Jeffrey

  Ryan

   Stella

   Luna

  Kailey

  Hayden Thomas Honolka

 Suzanne Kay Dudek

Vlasta (Patricia) Honolka

 Daniel (Dan) Dennis Grimm

 David (Dave) Dean Grimm

John Honolka, Jr.   DOB: 6/8/1946   DOD: 11/22/2020
   Susan Renee Honolka Missimo
      Gabriella (Gabby) Suzanne Missimo
      Alexis (Lexi) Danielle Missimo
   Danny Wade Honolka
      Cayden Ragan Honolka
      Carson William Honolka
Tomas (Tom) Jaromir Honolka
   Benjamin (Ben) Joseph Honolka
      Lyndsay Michelle Honolka
         Maddox Rose Keown
         Milo Hawkins-Lee Keown
      Logan Benjamin Honolka
      Landon Benjamin Honolka
      Lawson Benjamin Honolka
   Andrea (Angie) Honolka
      Devon Kane Gautney
      Piper Marie Gautney
      Zoe Anne Elizabeth Gallegos
   Beau Tomas Honolka
   Cody Leon Honolka   DOB: 04/27/1988   DOD: 12/24/2011

SURVIVING WORLD WAR II

1939 – 1944 Trutnov to Nova' Paka, and back to Trutnov

Written by Eva Honolka Newman

THE SECOND WORLD WAR LEFT a deep imprint on my memory and many questions as a child. The emotion of fear daily was a constant companion. I was afraid to go to school because when the bombings came, and we were rushed into the basement crying of fear. When the bombs fell, the earth would shake – the glass windows would fall out and we never knew if we were going to be buried alive.

My mom always made the sign of the cross on our forehead for God's protection, to come safely home. When all was clear the teachers directed us back to our classrooms, dismissed classes, and sent us home. We sat there not moving – some crying, afraid to go home because bombs have no conscience. We knew some of us would not find a home or parents and worst of all we would be picked up by the people that would decide if we were worth saving. If you had blonde hair and blue eyes your chances were good to be adopted out to a family that was the personification of Hitler's perfect race.

Groceries were scarce and we had food stamps that specified portions of food: ½ lb. of meat per person a month, one dozen eggs, some milk, some flour, etc. Once or twice a month our home would be inspected, to check our pantry to see if we were buying groceries as dictated by the food stamps.

To own a radio was forbidden. To be informed was not encouraged. To listen to England and Prime Minister Churchill to find out how the war situation was going was a deadly step.

On a regular basis there were bonfires in our communities to burn books: the classics and the inspirational lift to the human spirit. Most of all in the line of fire was the black book; (the Bible) there was no need to believe in something nobody has seen, to get ideas of fairness and hope when the Government was meeting all your needs. A perfect race was being built, mentally and physically and the rest rightfully would be exterminated. No hindrance to the progress of this genealogy of perfect blonde, blue eyed humans.

Unknown to us, anytime of day or night there could be an inspection. A forceful knock on the door. Two Nazi Officers and a German Shepherd. A line up of all family members against a wall with hands behind you and a police dog in front of you. Any slight move and the trained dog were ready to attack and bite.

The two German Officers would roam through our home: checking drawers, lifting mattresses, looking for that black book and a radio.

In the attic, between the rafters was the Bible and a radio. On certain days, my Dad and a few of his friends would meet in our basement; with windows tightly sealed so light could not leak through. The men used candles; electricity was forbidden after nine o'clock at night. The group of friends huddled around the radio to tune into England and Prime Minister Churchill's confident voice to "never, never, never give up". The Bible was close at hand and words of hope, courage, faith, and strength were read. After that, everybody snuck out and went home; always careful not to be seen by anyone. Curfew in the street was 9 o'clock p.m. If you were caught you would be severely reprimanded. The precious Bible and radio were hidden again in the attic until the next secret meeting.

Since produce was scarce, the farmers formed a black market. If they had some extra food – the news spread through the grapevine and if a person were brave enough to sneak out of their home after nine pm extra food could be purchased at a risk of being found. My Father received a tip that a farmer had slaughtered a cow and had some extra meat. My Father went to the farmers house and purchased what was available which was precious as gold.

The meat was stored in our pantry. The pantry was in a room without windows to keep it dark and cool. There were no ice boxes.

The next morning the unthinkable came to pass. Early morning, 5 AM, a knock at the door. We knew the routine. We lined up against the wall with hands behind you and a dog in front of us. The search took place continuing to the attic. To this day I can relive the fear, anxiety, and horror of what would happen if the Bible and radio were found. My fidgeting made the dog growl and show his teeth. My 6-year-old mind kept asking "Why"? What were we guilty of? We passed the inspection and now the food stamps were handed over for the Officers to check the pantry to see if we were on track with our food. My hair stood on top of my head – oh my God – we were forbidden meat in our pantry.

In no time at all, one of the Officer's came and grabbed my Father. "Where did you purchase that meat"? A gun was placed at my Father's temple. Mother begged my Dad to reveal the information to save himself for the children. At that time there were 3 of us. I was born in 1937, my brother (Don) Vladimir in 1939 and my sister (Patricia) in 1942.

My father wept and the officers took him to the farmers' house. The family was ordered out of the home, marched to the barn in the back. In front of my father and the farmers family – that man was hung. My father always remembered that because we wanted to eat more. A man had to die, and my dad felt a deep source of guilt. The decision to save himself for his children – or keep silent was a cross he carried all his life. How cruel to control humanity with the amount of food they could eat.

In the summer we would raise vegetables and fruit gardens to supplement our produce. The jars of preserves my mother hid in the coal bin in the basement. I loved the poppy seed patch. Mom made many wonderful pastries with poppy seed filling. I always had a craving to go to the patch and break off the poppy seed pods and indulge myself. I had a great deal of energy and became a wild hare.

Worst of all I broke the poppy when they were green and very bitter which appealed to my palate and made me feel good, gave me courage to climb tall trees. My mother sewed me beautiful pinafores to wear. In those days you owned two dresses and over the dresses I wore a different pinafore each day. The pattern was like an apron with big ruffles on the shoulders that looked like wings and a big ribbon around the waist that tied in the back.

I would come down from the tree to go home, ribbon dragging behind me, wings torn off my shoulders and my mom's voice "It would be better to have 10 boys than one girl" was my greeting.

To my father's dismay he wondered who was breaking the poppy's? In due time, he found out and I could not sit on my blessed assurance for a while. Green poppy's ????? and that was my energy drive that my father put a cubage on and saved the lovely pinafores my mother so patiently and perfectly sewed.

The German occupation of the Sudetenland made life intolerable for the Czech population. Friendships of long standing, business relationships, even marriages, were poisoned by an atmosphere of arrogance, intolerance, and tyranny, perpetrated by people we once had called our neighbors and friends.

Many Czech individuals and families, finding that the "New Order" had brought with it a dark night in the soul of the Czech nation, chose to leave. Homes, farms, businesses, so long, and so well cared for, were simply abandoned as their former owners sought respite from the depredations of the New Order in the Sudetenland.

Although a permit to travel was required from the German authorities, many Czechs simply left without observing the required formalities. The family of Jan Honolka was one such family.

Early on a Sunday morning, my Mother Jarmila packed diapers, clothing, and a lunch into a baby buggy and took me on a Sunday walk. The walk took place under the unsuspecting noses of the German authorities and did not end until we arrived in Nova Paka some eighty miles from our former home in Trutnov.

I do not recall the details of our journey, nor of the early days of our lives in Nova Paka, my admittedly scant memory is aided by anecdotal stories of the time, told by both my Mother and Father.

In truth, our respite from the Germans was indeed brief, as they occupied the remainder of the Czech lands of Bohemia and Moravia in March of 1939. The neighboring region of Slovakia was governed by a collaborationist regime under the infamous Monsignor Tiso. With the occupation of the Czech lands, the Protectorate of Bohemia and Moravia was proclaimed by the Germans and our lives were changed forever.

It was while living in Nova Paka, and in the newly proclaimed "Protectorate" that our family was exposed to, and experienced firsthand, a degree of the tyranny and oppression our new "protectors" were capable of imposing.

Our home was often, in fact, you might say routinely, searched by the German police. The "New Order" had no need for a God, so therefore the Bible was fantasy of hope. Works of recognized and renowned literature were also seized and routinely burned in the town square, where all were required to watch.

Hunger was also a daily companion and was also a means by which our new "protectors" could control the population. Pantries and food storage areas were also subject to the searched for contraband.

Since hunger was our daily companion, the farmers in the area formed what is commonly called a "Black Market". Whenever they had some extra produce or meat, even eggs, word was circulated around through the "grapevine" that extra food was available.

Still, and because of the ever-present hunger, there were those brave enough, or perhaps desperate enough to risk arrest, to obtain extra food. My Father slipped out of our home and purchased a cow's stomach. Yes, all parts of an animal were used.

The main meal we were able to purchase at the meat market was horse meat, which was extremely hard and muscular. In contrast, the cow's stomach was a delicacy. My Mother would cut the stomach into long strips which resembled noodles in appearance. With this, my Mother would then cook a soup called Drskova Polivaka. During this time, I choose to either be ill or play "Tinker Bell" and simply disappear. In my mind it was better to be hungry than to eat THAT.

Another article that the police were especially interested in were radios. Radios were especially dangerous in the eyes of the authorities, as one might listen to the BBC, and hear the defiant, but often reassuring voice of Winston Churchill. Of course, in the minds of our "protectors" listening to what was the truth was detrimental to our health and mental well-being.

Still, and despite the incipient terror and loss of liberty brought on by the occupation, the human spirit that indomitable force, which is the creation of an Almighty God, remained with us. It was in Nova Paka that my sense of wonder, my curiosity, my sense of things beautiful and unchanging was born and began to take shape.

It is by nature, and in the majesty of God's creation, the Czech lands are set in some of the most beautiful country on the face of the earth. Towering mountains, verdant plains with rich soil, rushing streams, and lakes, a veritable paradise on earth. Not even the Germans with all their arrogance, and the totally evil spirit of their intentions could compromise the beauty of the land or the spirit of the Czech people whom they sought to dominate.

My favorite playtime in the Spring was to play "Princess of the Meadow". This was when the dandelions (Pampelisky) bloomed. Out of these, I would make wreaths to place on my head, and both necklaces and bracelets, and even a ring. I felt like a "Sun Goddess", and my imagination allowed me to be in a world of beauty.

Nature had a profound effect of wonder on my soul, the touch of the infinite was around me even though I had nothing to compare my feelings to: (Churches were locked there was no God).

As I Lay on my back in the meadow – looking into what universe – imagination carried me to joy, peace, calm – here I was safe. Living in fear as a child, I found stillness of nature pure and good and my heart rejoiced at the sense of serenity and awe. The vast heaven beckoned to me to search for the peace that passed all understanding.

When the wildflowers bloomed, I always gathered a bouquet for my Mother and proudly I presented to her the flowers to show my love and appreciation.

My Mother, a brilliant, talented soul, and still much filled with the exuberance of youth, was my companion and guide as I began my journey and quest to seek the beauty of nature, and to appreciate the force for good that it would be in my life. Thus, I began a journey of inquiry and delight, one I still pursue to this day during 2019. My inner drive remains with me. I had, and still have that irresistible force which compels me into no uncertain terms to accomplish big things. Things both large and small.

This need to accomplish, to complete a given mission as it were, could be as simple as sewing clothes for a doll, looking for a pattern with my all-encouraging Mother, reading books which enthralled me, and which were a vertical window on the world.

I trilled and marveled at the prospect the challenge of athletics. Skiing, water sports, ice skating. I was obsessed with the piano, and in vivid dreams I would see my fingers caressing the keyboard as I played Dvorak's New World Symphony or explored the works of Smetana or Mozart.

Yet, my biggest thrill was the ballet. This superbly athletic and disciplined combination of beauty and art, all combined to produce a most magical and profoundly beautiful form of human expression. It was this drive, this vision, this spirit, both born and nurtured in the town of Nova Paka, which late led to my receiving a scholarship to the Art Institute of Chicago, Illinois. A place which so dramatically represented a totally different life than the one I have described thus far.

By now it was early 1945, and the war, so interminably long, was winding down. The roads to Europe were filled with the advancing allied armies of both the East and the West, and roads were filled with those caught up in the vacuum of war, the now displaced and homeless persons.

Still the relief from the falling bombs, the struggle of opposing armies was coming to an end, but not before the presence of the advancing Russian Army made itself felt in our lives.

1945 Koruna Fancy Pastries

The War Ended
Written by Eva Honolka Newman

MY FATHER HAD BEEN THE manager of a chocolate factory in his native Czechoslovakia before and during WWII, but there was always the gnawing desire to enter business for himself – to become an owner in his own right. He had his own ideas about building his wafer company. With the most up to date facilities and equipment, coupled with a progressive, fair, and democratic manner of doing business, his company prospered.

This ambition was realized in 1945 at the close of the war when he established Koruna Fancy Pastries in Pilnikov, Czechoslovakia. Pihikov was close to our hometown of Trutnov. He delivered his Oplatky all over Czechoslovakia. Oplatky was is dessert made of many thin layers of dough filled with cream fillings, nuts, chocolate, caramel, and sugar. It was a popular afternoon treat with coffee or tea.

In mere months, his success was assured. In less than three years the business was booming. He had become what he had always wanted to be – a man with an idea that had found its' time and was now a tangible, working reality that provided jobs for assistants, delectable treats for his customers, and the good things of life for his family.

His world was the best it had ever been. His fundamental traits of willingness to take a risk, devote personal initiate, self-reliance and hard work had paid off.

The love of business, and his care and concern for his 25 employees were nothing less than awesome. He passionately believed in assisting his employees to build better lives, and to share in the good fortunes of the company they built.

He was keenly aware of the sufferings not only he and our family endured under the Nazis, but of the sufferings of so many of his employees and their families as well.

My Dad was his own hardest critic. This quality was born of his athleticism, his upbringing, his perfectionism, and his profound belief in not merely doing things well, but with a high degree of perfectionism. He analyzed and criticized himself long before he took others to task.

In 1947, Once again, Jan Honolka's resolve and determination were tested, when lighting struck the factory burning it to the ground.

Largely due to a well-deserved reputation for honesty and integrity, a bank loaned my Father the money to begin once more. The word "quit" either in Czech, German, or English, was never in our father's vocabulary. Even though all his savings had been lost in the fire, Jan Honolka resolved to begin once again, from scratch. Mission was accomplished.

The business prospered. People were happy the war was over. We all were grateful to the American soldiers for their kind behavior, always having a smile and lending a helpful hand. Who could forget chewing gum, candy, and nylons for the ladies? Such generosity was not familiar to us. General Patton came in, with his 3rd Army and our love and respect for America became infectious.

1948 Beginning of Communism

Written by Eva Honolka Newman

The signs of problems were soon evident, and a new fear gripped our hearts, good God, another conflict?

General Patton made a strong appeal when there was a meeting of Military Officers in Prague; "Put the Soviet Military back in Russia before we leave Europe". Of course, that advice was disregarded; the rest is history − 40 years of Communism, oppression, and the loss of freedom.

The decision was made in 1948 election as to whether the people were to elect Democracy or Communism. There was the big propaganda promise that Communism would bring this paradise/utopia, free medicine, great social welfare, handouts from Mother government, an individual would no longer be responsible for himself or his own welfare. A blissful society of everyone equal and the promise that hard work gave more dignity and freedom, in exchanged the government supervised.

After the 6 years of the war, the horror of concentration camps − this indeed sounded like a gift from heaven. The tired and worn-out Czech people glued themselves to this new promise and the rest is history.

Of course, there was that certain percentage of the Czech society that knew the consequences of electing communism. As hard as they tried, they soon realized we have a new war, a silent war, a political war.

A coop society was formed, businesses were nationalized, prosperity confiscated. If you were not willing to be indoctrinated your fate in life was sealed, servant of the State. Wow − slavery.

With the re-structuring of the new coop society − many things were changing, and with change comes confusion.

The order was given that anyone who had some German background, regardless of how long they had lived in Czechoslovakia had to be thrown out because of the atrocities the Nazis committed in our country. Age was of no consideration. My father's father was Austrian, his mom was half German. They were the second generation living in Trutnov. They could pack 60 Kilos, approximately 132 pounds of possessions per person. A government truck picked them up and they were whisked away into the unknown. News came many weeks later that they relocated in a two-room apartment in Berchtesgaden, Germany. Two senior citizens totally lost and guilty of nothing. War is hell.

The Russians took over where the Germans left off. Most soldiers were from the primitive and poor of Russia. They pillaged, raped, and abused our population.

If any person has a watch it would be confiscated, some soldiers wore many watches on their arms.

Behind our home was a large meadow, where the Russian military setup a large camp. In the evenings large bonfires were lit; the soldiers danced the Kozak dances and sand haunting melodies, drank vodka, and tied their horses to trees. They teased them with sticks until the animals foamed at their mouths. In their aggravated condition the soldiers jumped on the horses and rode them like bulls at a rodeo.

The tirade went on until early morning hours and with the break of dawn quiet fell upon the field, just to start all over the next night.

We were ordered that once a week we had to host Russian officers. A formal dinner was prepared. We were instructed to socialize with the officers, drink their vodka and celebrate victory over Germany. My Mother's sister was allergic to liquor and when she refused to drink, that was an insult to the officers. She was forced to partake in the cheers. Soon, she became ill, and fell into a coma.

Our guests found this to be very humorous and we had a difficult time getting her to the hospital. In her unconscious state she was a perfect subject for rape. Fortunately, the ambulance arrived in time and in due time she fully recovered.

Getting to Know John Honolka, Sr.

Written by Eva Honolka Newman

I wish you would have known my father personally; but before this story is done, you will know him better and hopefully will be the better for the knowledge.

He was not a native-born American, but he taught all of us who are natives what our role as such should be. Entertain no doubt about it, he was American to the core. And here we speak in the connotation of the sense in which that word was originally applied.

The breed that I am thinking about are worse. In fact, because they, all above all other citizens should appreciate and defend the values of free enterprise and self-reliance. Yet, all too often they seek bailouts, federal favors, or regulatory protection conferring competitive advantage. Dad knew better. He would make no such requests and indulge in no such practices, because he, of all people knew all too well that whenever government is structured and encouraged to play the role of "Helping Hand", then sooner or later it OWNS YOU. This was the very thing from which he had boldly and successfully fought, though not without terrible cost.

But hadn't you heard, John Honolka? These things are discouraged when applied to your own interests – especially business interest. In those nations whose governments tended towards a collective bend, and John, one day when you were not looking your elected representatives in Parliament were shouted down and displaced by a minority of collectivists of the worst stripe, and your government was taken over by the communists.

Suddenly, without your hardly realizing it, black was white, night was day, dark was light, and all your good traits were just so many dead weights for now. You are a capitalist in a Communist land. The worst label with which you could be tagged.

Overnight you were is a different atmosphere. Friends became distrustful, brothers turned against brothers, and neighbors against neighbors. Even the children were drawn into the controversy. Incredible, you may have thought, until the incident of your little daughter, Eva, brought it straight home to you.

As children will do at times, be children invoking name-calling. Eva, during an exchange with a neighbor child one day resorted to the most demeaning title her little thought process could conjure up – "You – you Communist, you."

Father was released after a warning against teaching such attitudes to his offspring, doubtless he was not only astonished, but shaken as well. Bear in mind this was in Czechoslovakia. Which had been the Central European Showcase of Democracy between World Wars. How has nation been in the throes of totalitarian take over whose instrument of control was terror.

It was during this general period in 1948 that my Dad fell victim to an extended illness brought on by chronic throat infections which in turn led to a three week stay in the hospital. Therefore, being absence from Koruna Fancy Pastries.

He returned to a far different world.

While no money had exchanged hands, yet a man was seated at this desk who informed him that his business had been nationalized and now belonged to the state.

"No man should own so much, or control these many workers," he was told. "This is permitted only by the state."

One wonders if it dawned on my dad that moment the fallacy that is contained in such and assertion. Where on earth did mankind get the mistaken notion that a so called "Crime" perpetrated by an individual is any less a criminal act when committed by the government?

Indeed, this is the measure by which all outrages against individual liberty and abuse of power by government should be defined.

As Frederic Bastiat so aptly put it: See if this act (of government) benefits one citizen (group of citizens or business) at the expense of another (citizen, group of citizens of business) by doing what the benefited citizen himself cannot do without committing a crime.

This is the standard which must be applied to all official acts affecting life, liberty, and property if government is to be kept in its proper place and perform its rightful role, that of preventing injustice from overtaking even one citizen that another or others might be enriched.

It is, of course, the antithesis of this philosophy which confiscated Koruna Fancy Pastries and made John Honolka an "enemy" of the "People".

He could, of course, redeem himself, he was told, if he chose to lend his status (of which he had his share) in the community to the Communism Party. By joining and working in the interest of its aims and goals, which in theory words was to "establish a great new society in the land".

How he must have been appalled in later years, after he reached these shores of the United States of America to hear these same words "Great society" spoken in all seriousness by an American President as descriptive of the goal to which his administration aspired.

We forget: Government is not omnipotent; only God is. "Just join us, the Communists cooed "and we will work together for the betterment of all". It is to be noted that not once was there a call for a great re-awakening of the human spirit.

They even offered to let him stay on with the business as its manager. How generous. To remain as manager of what once had been his own imagination and initiative – how generous, indeed.

He rejected their sleazy bribe, hands down, and in that act became a marked man. This was on a Saturday. It has been said that the "mills of the gods grind slowly."

Not so, the machinery of Atheistic Marxism. The following day, Sunday, he took the family for a walk in the park and there in their presence was arrested for "illegal activities against his government, and not cooperating to the best interests of society and the state.

His real crime, of course, was that he was simply a capitalist by philosophy and practice. A Naboth who only wanted his vineyard and that which was his own.

Our mother was questioned and her feelings about the government and explored the general status of her attitude towards the new regime. She was informed that her husband would be kept in custody and made to labor in the coal mines until he was "re-educated".

Jailed for two months in his own hometown. Indoctrinated daily; until a problem came up at the business. This happened often when a business was nationalized and placed in the hands of incompetents.

Our father would be released if he would assist in the alleviation of the problem. Oh. – "All knowing" torturers, are you not aware that this John Honolka whom you made your victim was also a man, even as each of you, with intelligence, the faculty to observe, to know, to think, to plan and to judge for himself; else why did you call him back to his post?

He bowed at their shrine only long enough to escape it.

With the help of the underground, he made his way to Vienna only to turn back to rescue his family. But this time he was caught just before crossing the border back into Austria. The family remained separated for nine months.

During this period father was sentenced to three months in hard labor – more accurately hard abuse at the hands of the Communist attempt to "re-educate" him again. He was strung up by his wrists, beaten with heavy leather straps until his back was scarred for life. A mute testimony to one man's conviction that human dignity is preserved only if the spirit is permitted to run free.

"What is so bad about the Communist Party"? he was asked of so reasonably. John answered, "it stunts individual liberty and personal development". He might have added; it dehumanizes and enslaves; and therefore, our founding fathers knew it is government which must be restrained and kept within bounds – not bodies and souls which should be manacled.

Our father's spirit remained free and after nine months his body was free also having made good another escape and with the aid of the American Red Cross was reunited with his family. He had lost track of them completely; in the French Sector of Austria, the city of Salzburg to be exact.

The ordeal and accompanying deprivations (and there were many for the Honolka Family) as it waited out three long years in the Displaced Persons Camps and their agonizingly slow success in finally being accepted by a sympathetic country is a story to go to itself. Suffice it to say that they did make it out of Europe; having been slated to go to New Zealand, but at the last minute switched to America and on to a new life.

COMING TO AMERICA

1951 Bremerhaven, Germany, to New Orleans, LA, to Protivin, IA

Written by Eva Honolka Newman

MY FATHER WAS OBSESSED WITH the hope of emigrating to America, the land of freedom and opportunity. We talked about it, we dreamed about it, we fantasized about, and we prayed for it to happen.

We had walked away from our home, our family, our friends, and our roots, with only the clothes on our backs, in search of freedom.

In 1951 we had a sponsor and approval to go the U.S.A. We went by ship, the USNS General Harry Taylor. Our 3-week trip landed in New Orleans. We took a train to Cresco, Iowa where we were met by our American sponsor, a corn farmer (Frank Kostohryz) and his wife, Marie. We rode to our new "Home" in Protivin, Iowa on the back of a flatbed truck. Protivin, Iowa was founded by Czech settlers in mid-19th century.

"Home" was an old weather-beaten farmhouse that the cows lived in during the winter months. There was no running water, toilet facilities, gas, or electricity in the house, but there was an outhouse and a water well outside. The basement was full of water, and we had to shovel the "Cow chips" out of the house before we could even live there. All we could see for miles in every direction was 500 acres of barren fields, to

be plowed, planted, and cultivated, and our family was brought here to do that in return for our passage from Germany.

There is no way I can relate to you exactly how it felt when we arrived at our destination, even though it was America and freedom. We had all imagined, hoped, and dreamed of luxurious surroundings, a nice home, a nice car, and a golden opportunity. We stood back, in shock, with the reality of our situation. We had nothing, we came there destitute, obligated, broken, torn, anxious and hungry. We had no means of transportation and the nearest farm was miles and miles away. We were almost like indentured servants. We asked ourselves "What now"? We could not go back to the camps, we were stuck. The situation was so bad that it broke my Mother's heart, partly because she came from a very classy family. It was such a disappointment to her that she never really ever got over it."

My Dad, John Honolka, was an honorable man, trustworthy, tenacious, a hard master, disciplined, and a dedicated parent. He was my role model. He once shared his philosophy of work with me, he said "An aggressive man will work today and play tomorrow, but a lazy man will play today and work tomorrow. A twelve-hour day is only a half day's work."

We stuck it out on the farm that summer of 1951, but we knew we could not survive a northern Iowa winter under those austere conditions.

With the help of the Chamber of Commerce in Cedar Rapids, and the Milo Maxera family, we moved to Cedar Rapids, worked, and attended school. Dad worked two or three jobs to support his family of five children. We all did our share working hard and long hours.

John Honolka's big opportunity finally came in 1955 when he was hired to manage the Amana Bakery at the Amana Colonies in Amana, Iowa. He built the business into a thriving, productive, and profitable million-dollar operation. He increased sales almost 1,000 percent by 1966.

At the peak of production, the bakery distributed bread in eight states in the Midwest, via refrigerated trucks. It was his innovative approach which took the loaves out of the waxed paper and put them in the now familiar poly bags for greater convenience, freshness, and product visibility.

He found that the streets of America were paved with gold, but the gold was freedom, liberty, and opportunity. All of us became Naturalized American Citizens. None of us became rich and famous but we all have lived to realize the American dream, have become successful, and enjoyed over 68 years of freedom.

John Honolka lived 32 years to the day, after having arrived in New Orleans on 26 April 1951. America is the better place for that 32 years, for he lived as he believed; that there is gold in the streets of America if you are not too lazy to bend over and pick it up. It lies in the promise that American offers to work as a free man and pursue happiness with hope.

Dad was not too lazy to bend over. In fact during his first four years in America with no proof of his education and work background he had to take what came; two jobs as a janitor, one job as a butcher and one as a supermarket clerk, in the produce department. He performed all four jobs every day, six days per week, beginning at 5:00 am until 10:00 pm at night but his pursuit of happiness with hope paid off. He once again became a successful businessman.

What lesson does John Honolka hold for the average American businessman? This is my approximate conclusion:

The lesson lies in recognizing the value of a personal incentive that will reach out and take hold of the opportunities provided by Freedom as we have known it in America; but that Freedom must be guarded. You do not take it for granted. Therefore, you do not, you must not ignore those indiscretions of government which would immobilize the opportunities it provides.

A wayward government must be kicked in line more swiftly than a wayward person who tries to rob you of your liberty, for unlike John Honolka, you may not get a second chance.

John Honolka was a worthy man made for acceptance into the American Community.

AMERICA IS THE LAND OF OPPORTUNITY

In August of 1992, Don and Sharon began a trip through Iowa to explore the past which included the arrival of John Honolka and his family to the United States of America.

Their first stop was to find the family of their sponsor Frank Kostohryz. Adela Kostohryz said, "My father-in-law ran an ad in the newspaper for employees". "The home has not been occupied since the Honolka's left in the Fall of 1951 because the home remains with no running water or electricity and the winters are very harsh in North East Iowa".

Looking through the windows, Don sees a remaining rocking chair used by the entire family.

In the back we find the water pump next to the cow tank. The cow tank was multi-functional. It served as a bathing tub, swimming pool, clothes washer, and cow tank.

It was not unusual to walk five miles to the grocery store in Protivin. Don said, "The store looks the same in 1992 as if it did in 1951. Same wooden floors and ceilings – Operated by the Third Generation".

As we toured town, Mr. Verba shared with Don the first time John Honolka asked for "Parky" also known as "Hot Dogs".

The Honolka family often purchased meat from Polashek's Locker in Provitin.

We went from grocery stores and meat lockers to find Mary Hudecek and her beautiful white house. Mrs. Hudecek spoke extremely highly of Jarmila Honolka, referring to her as a "Very classy city girl".

Poor living and working conditions forced the family from Protivin to Cedar Rapids during the late Fall of 1951. John Honolka held multiple jobs to support his large family. His primary job was held at the Kapoun and Polehna Meat Market.

I was enormously proud of my husband, Don Honolka, during this 1992 trip. He wanted me to learn a portion of his history. I was amazed that he openly and freely went to hunt down his past. Who would have ever known that 28 years later I would be pulling out photo albums that contained documented notes?

What Were The "Honolka's"?

Refugee or Immigrant

Refugee – A person who has been forced to leave their country to escape war, persecution, or natural disaster. A refugee has a well-founded fear of persecution for reasons of race, religion, nationality, political opinion, or membership in a particular social group. The United States has long been a global leader in the resettlement of refugees – and the need for such leadership remains enormous.

Immigrant – A person who comes to live permanently in a foreign country. Foreign citizens who want to live permanently in the United States must first obtain an immigrant visa. This is the first step to becoming a lawful permanent citizenship.

Current steps to becoming a naturalized American.

1. Obtain a green card.

The first step to naturalization is to obtain a green card and maintain residence in the country for five years, according to the U.S. Citizenship and Immigration Services.

2. Maintain a physical presence.

Immigrants must be physically present in the country for 30 months of the five years needed to apply for citizenship. Applicants also must live within the state or USCIS district with jurisdiction over the applicant's place of residence for at least three months before applying.

3. Complete the USCIS form N-400.

Petitioners fill out their background information on the form, which also enables them to do things like have a legal name change. Applying is not cheap, however. Completing the form costs $595 and an additional $85 biometrics fee, according to Law.

4. Be fingerprinted.

Once the application is accepted, a date will be set for fingerprinting and biometrics at a local office. These will be used to perform a background check done by the Federal Bureau of Investigation.

5. Pass the interview and naturalization test.

An appointment will be made with a USCIC officer for an interview to review the N-400 form and answer questions the petitioner may have. The examination requires those who wish to become citizens to understand English as well as civics, including U.S. history and government. There are some exemptions and waivers. Participants are given two chances to the pass the test.

REGARDLESS
The "Honolka's"
Became Naturalized Citizens
April 9, 1957

1955 No Bitterness in Heart of Czech DP Teen-Ager

Cedar Rapids Gazette
January 16, 1955
By: Russ Wiley, Gazette Staff Writer

Eva Honolka, 17, is free to select a book of her choice from the library at St. Wenceslaus high school. That freedom is part of the reward she and her family won by escaping from Communist-controlled Czechoslovakia.

Trouble-tossed teen-age years as a Czech displaced person might well have taught only lessons of bitterness and hatred to 17-year-old Eva Honolka.

But Eva safe today in Cedar Rapids, Iowa would rather talk about youthful responsibilities in character building and about the unexplored areas of man's love for fellow man.

Eva may seem a little critical of some of the things she sees going on around her in America. But that criticism is understood when you know all of Eva's story.

Having a party dress is nice. But Eva has known the years when just a spark of hope seemed awfully big.

"Girls here say clothes make the girl. If you buy beautiful clothes, you will be beautiful.

That is wrong. The first thing is to build good character. Then you will be pretty.

Another thing," added Eva, Lots of money and fun. That is all you hear. So many American boys and girls spend all their money on clothes and fun. "Why don't they take a dollar or two every week and give it to people that need it more than they do".

Eva likes her classes at St. Wenceslaus. She lives with her family in a southwest side home. She loves music, dancing, and art, although artwork is the only one, she is financially able to practice.

It was not like that for Eva and the Honolka's five years ago.

They were part of the world's lowliest peoples during the post war period in Europe; they bore the dubious label of DP'S – Displaced Person

They had merger belongings little and sometimes nothing to eat. Most important, they had no home, other than the one they had escaped from in Czechoslovakia.

The family was separated for many months. The mother and children not knowing the whereabouts of their husband and father. They were shifted continually among Communist prison camps and European Displaced Person camps.

About the only thing they owned was freedom – Before the war they had more than enough to live comfortably. The head of the family, John Honolka, was successfully operating his own food processing plant in Czechoslovakia. Mrs. Honolka also and art and music lover, used to take little Eva to concerts where they watched Europe's greatest artists perform.

Eva dreamed of becoming a ballet dancer and pianist.

"My mother was planning to send me to ballet school and buy a piano. I was 12 years old. But suddenly we had lost everything, and we were trying to escape," said Eva, whose English is remarkable, even distinctive with its slight accent.

The following two years live in Eva's memory as a rapid, confusing jumble of horrors and fears. She will talk about those memories, but you can see she'd rather talk about things like American girls and boys who spend all their money on clothes and fun instead of giving some of it to less fortunate people.

"The people who have everything and don't have to work hard for it are the ones who will turn to communism if it ever comes here," she said.

"That's what happened in Czechoslovakia.

"Many wealthy people joined with the Communists because they were afraid to lose everything. They didn't know what else to do, because they had never known what it was to provide for themselves."

"Not my Father" – Without saying so, Eva plainly showed that she is proud that her father was not among that kind of people.

She shook her head and said, "My father, well, he just didn't want to live that way.

"If he had chosen to stay in Czechoslovakia after the Communists took over his factory, we could still be there as wealthy people."

Today in Cedar Rapids, John Honolka, a college graduate works as a clerk in the Daniel's park grocery store. He still yearns to enter bigger business, Eva said, on a scale like his position in the old country.

And here is the Honolka family story:

"Years ago, my father earned a living by skiing and playing hockey and football." Said Eva. During the war, he was manager of a chocolate factory. After the war he started his own factory, making ready-to-eat waffles. He had 25 employees.

"While his business was at its best, he had to have his tonsils taken out. Without his knowledge, the Communists suddenly took over his factory while he was in the hospital.

"When he went back to work, two men met him and told him the factory didn't belong to him anymore. The state owned it. He could work there as manager and continue to have a nice living if he would join the party.

"My Daddy refused."

"Then one Sunday he and my brother, Johnny who is eight now, were walking in the park. Two men arrested him and said he could have one week to get his affairs in order before being sent somewhere to work in the coal mines.

"My Daddy spent the week planning his escape. He left, alone, and later came back for the rest of us." At that time there was Eva, her, brothers, Lada (Don), now 15, and Johnny, and sister Vlasta (Patricia), now 12.

Daddy hired two men from the Underground, and they took us to Hungry. Two more men took us to the Austrian Border where a woman was supposed to help us.

She wanted to see our papers, though, and of course we did not have any because we were escaping.

When my father asked a taxi driver to take us back to Budapest, the driver told two Communist police that we were escaping. They arrested us.

Then came a succession of "One jail and prison after another, and finally, our Daddy was separated from us.

He was beaten. He still has scars on his back.

In one prison, Mrs. Honolka, who had some college work, who had once owned beautiful paintings and played the violin, lived a different life. She and the four children had to live for three months in a big hall with about 500 other prisoners, all women, and children.

We ate a red pepper and piece of dark bread each day. Sometimes they gave us a hot water soup. The children never had milk. The children cried day and night.

Johnny became quite sick and Mother almost had a nervous breakdown. I still have scars on my skin from scratching off insects.

All that time we knew nothing about Daddy.

After that they were sent to Germany and Vienna. "My Mother still had some jewelry, so she sold it and hired an Underground agent to take us to the American zone.

The mother and children ended up in a displaced persons camp in Salzburg, a camp that was in awful condition. The remainder of Mrs. Honolka's jewelry and money was stolen, and the police didn't do anything because we were displaced persons and didn't belong to the country.

Finally, while Eva slept one morning, a man walked into their quarters in the Displaced Persons camp. "I woke up, looked at the man, and didn't even recognize my own father," said Eva.

"You can't realize how time and conditions can change the expression on a man's face. You know, when someone is scared, his eyes go wide open. That's how Daddy's eyes looked."

The family, together again, was later transferred to another Displaced Persons camp. "It was much better because it was supported by Americans. We got CARE packages from America.

"Father started to write to America and a New York family sent us money and packages. It was just wonderful."

An opportunity came for Eva, Lada (Don) and Vlasta (Patricia) to enter a home for children in Switzerland. From there, Lada and Eva were adopted by separate families. But after six months, they returned to Germany.

"In 1949 we were all ready to immigrate to Norway. But then Tommy (now 5) was born." At this point Eva lowered her head a bit. "So, my littlest brother was born in a Displaced Persons camp."

Mr. Honolka then started making out papers for entry into Austria, New Zealand, and the United States. "The American acceptance came first. One of the happiest moments of our lives was the arrival of that news – happier than words can express."

The boat that brought them to America docked first in South America to leave 500 Displaced Persons to that country. Then they landed in New Orleans. "and, oh, that first look at America". The tall buildings and the language seemed so strange."

On a train trip to Chicago, Eva got sick from eating too much candy."

The Honolkas first settled on a farm near Cresco where their family sponsor, Frank Kostohrys, who died recently, lived. "We could not get use to farm life."

"Then some people in Cedar Rapids heard about us. They are Mr. and Mrs. Andrew Polehna, Mr. and Mrs. Robert P. Kapoun and Mr. and Mrs. Milo Maxera. They brought me here. I was 14 then."

"Later they found a house for the rest of the family in Walford and gave Daddy a job in their meat market. "On Saturdays, for a while, I worked at Milo Maxeras pastry shop.

"And finally, we found a house in Cedar Rapids. It is at 1507 Hamilton Street SW. My father did not like the butcher work, so got his job in the food market so he can do sales work, he still would rather do business work."

When Eva entered St. Wenceslaus school, she couldn't speak English. Lada chose Wilson High School, So he can go out for more sports." Vlasta (Patricia) and Johnny are also attending St. Wenceslaus.

What is ahead? "In two years," said Eva. I'll get my citizenship. That will be another big event in my life."

While she likes American and says, "I'm willing to work hard and want to do well here." Eva will always have a "longing to see the old country."

"To do well." Eva thinks it's twice as easy here in American as in Europe." Here, she says, all you have to do is show ability and interest and someone will help you."

A teacher sees that a student has talent and arranges a scholarship for him. There is nothing like that in Europe. Much talent and ability are wasted when those who have it are poor because no one cares.

Eva concluded:" All of us will never be able to repay or thank all the people that have helped us."

We are convinced. After listening to Eva, that all who helped the Honolkas are replying: "It was our pleasure."

1955 Former Czech Now Manages Amana Bakery

The Cedar Rapids Gazette, Sunday, September 25, 1955
By: Laurie Van Dyke, Staff Writer-Photographer

AMANA – A man imprisoned as a capitalist in his native Czechoslovakia has found his first satisfaction in America in this colony that turned down communal living in favor of capitalism.

John Honolka owned his own bakery in Trutnov, near the German-Polish border. Then came the Communist revolution in 1948 and three days later the bakery was wrested from him. He was thrown into prison, labeled a capitalist.

Honolka is not quite the capitalist in America that he was in Czechoslovakia. He does not even own his own bakery yet. But he is the new manager of the Amana colonies bakery in Upper South Amana.

The new bakery manager has the initiative to become an American capitalist. Only a short time after his entry into the country in 1951 he had written Chambers of Commerce all over the country about ways to get his bakery specialty, a German wafer, on the market.

The anomaly of having a Czech as manager of a bakery noted for its German products can be explained readily by the fact that Honolka lived in German Czechoslovakia. His bakery there produced fine German pastries.

"This is what I need." said Honolka after three months in his manager's job. "For the first time since I came to America I am very, very satisfied."

"For a young man to start over again in this country is quite easy. For an old man it's not so easy." said the 45-year-old Honolka.

If only we had come here 20 years ago," concurred his blonde wife, who has just recently moved family belongings into the upper story of the bakery building. "There's a lot more opportunity here than over there."

Young at Heart

The appearance of both the Honolka's bellies their talk about getting old. Their good humor is more in evidence than any regrets about the past.

Honolka does not waste time worrying about becoming a capitalist in this country. He has five children to feed and educate.

He would still like to get his German wafer, the Karlsbader, on the market, but the $2,000 the wafer machine would cost is too much to think about – he's more anxious to put his children through college.

Anything else is too far in the future.

"The main problem for me now is to give my children a good education and profession – that's all I want," said Honolka. "The main problem is to live as a free people in a free country."

The Honolka children are Eva, 18, Don, 16, Vlasta, 13, John, 9, and Tommy 5.

They were all born in Czechoslovakia except Tommy, born while his parents were refugees in Germany, and his father was working for the French secret police.

Screened Refugees

It was Honolka's job then to help screen refugees in Germany, to determine whether they were Communist spies or actual political refugees. He worked in Germany from the time of his escape in 1948 until his immigration in the United States in 1951.

Honolka spent three months in a forced labor camp in the coal mines before he managed the escape of himself and his family through the aid of a friend. The camp contained persons who had been businessmen and factory owners.

"They arrested me because they said, as they say for everybody. "He is a capitalist." The Czech recalled.

The family's sponsor in this country was a Czech farmer. Honolka worked on a farm as short time and then moved to Cedar Rapids.

He could not find a job in a bakery, so he worked for a sausage factory, since closed. Then he went to work in the meat department of the Daniels Park Foods, where he worked until he became manager of the Amana bakery three months ago. The bakery is owned by the Amana Society.

Hard Worker

Honolka worked up from the bottom to become owner of the bakery in his native land. The work was hard even after he was head man. Sometimes he worked from 3 in the morning until 10 at night.

Days are not so long for him here, though he is on the job seven days a week. The bakery has a staff of about 25 persons. The number increased somewhat since Honolka became manager.

He already has added two new products to the bakery's line, a new type of coffee cake and an all-rye bread. He hopes to add more products in the future.

A third bakery route, to Davenport, is to be added soon. Routes now are to Marshalltown and Newton and to Iowa City, Cedar Rapids and Manchester. In addition, there are special deliveries for all the Amana colonies.

Speaks Four Languages

When the Honolka's came to Cedar Rapids, they could speak little English and they sought friends who could speak their language. This could have been any one of several languages, since Honolka speaks Czech, German, Polish and French.

Someone told him to visit the Amanas. There were Germans there, he was told, who would talk German with him.

Honolka followed the suggestion and the family soon had friends in Amana, one of them Fred Geiger, manager of the general store in Main Amana. It was Geiger who told Honolka about the manager's job at the colony bakery and was instrumental in bringing him to Amana.

Upper story of the bakery building, red brick like most colony structures, was remodeled at one end into an apartment. The Honolkas moved in three weeks ago and the began attending classes at the school in Middle Amana.

The school bus stops in front of the bakery each morning. The four older children were St. Wenceslaus students in Cedar Rapids last year when the family lived at 1507 Hamilton Street SW Cedar Rapids, Iowa.

After school and on weekends the older children help in the bakery and Eva is head salesgirl on Saturdays.

Eva already has plans for her college education. Then there will be four more children to educate....... a task that would challenge even a capitalist.

1966 Bakery Production and Marketing Magazine

September 24, 1966, Volume 1 ★ No. 1

Bread loves in eight Midwestern states are becoming acquainted with a brand name that once was known in but an exceedingly small section of central Iowa.

The name is Amana – now appearing on several dozen varieties of specialty breads and rolls distributed from Kansas City to the Western counties of Illinois and Wisconsin… and from South Dakota to Missouri. Home base is the Amana Colonies, Amana, Iowa.

Expansion of the brand name and the product line traces back some 10 years. About, 1955, a desire on the part of the Amana Bakery to expand the commercial opportunities related to the talents of John Honolka, a baker recently arrived in the U. S. from the refugee camps of Europe. The marriage proved a happy one.

At that time, the Amana line of breads accounted for sales volume of approximately $9,000 per month. Sales figures are now running a better than $80,000 a month – and the prospects for a major improvement are well in sight.

Up to this point, Amana has been largely a small-town marketer. The only major markets exposed to the Amana brand have been Des Moines, Iowa and Omaha and Lincoln, Nebraska. But distribution (through local jobbers) is already arranged and citizens of both Kansas City and St. Louis, Mo., will be snacking on Amana label baked products this autumn. Chicago is in Honolka's plan as well.

Wholesale bakers in the area have been quick to appreciate the immediate and continued acceptance given to Amana's line of variety breads. Several have taken on the line jobbing Amana's products on their own wholesale routes, enabling Amana to realize the distribution economics of 'drop shipment" deliveries. This distribution factor, coupled with the fact that their one-pound varieties wholesale of 28 cents to 32 cents, explains why this Iowa enterprise nets a profit on sales of 3 to 4 percent.

The Amana product is a large selection of variety breads and rolls. Typical categories are round white, stone ground, caraway, farm bread, sour French, butter bread and several others. As many as 20 are offered at one time but Honolka is quick to add, "Customer preferences are always shifting. I watch sales carefully and am always ready to drop a style and replace with another as soon as demand drops," Honolka works with about a 25 per cent casualty list each year.

Honolka writes his own formulas – derived in part from his European background. His guide is selecting products is principally based on small 2-gallon market test with employees and perhaps a restaurant or two located conveniently to the bakery. The aim, typical of variety breads is to achieve a "home style" appearance.

The Amana Society Bakery is in South Amana in a distinctly rural setting. It is one among several that make up the Amana Colony.

Most of the region is familiar with the Colony because of the communal life principles which have guided the Colony for over 100 years. However, except for the location, brand name, and financing, there is no direct connection between the bakery and the Amana Colony. Neither Honolka nor most of his 35 employees are members of the Colony. His contractual obligation to the Colony is solely to operate a profitable wholesale bakery.

Honolka has developed his own job descriptions. He established sanitation, for example, as a part of the job pattern of each worker. Each person is held responsible for keeping his respective work area and machinery clean and sanitary at all times and is expected to plan his work schedule accordingly.

According to Honolka, an important contributor to Amana's sales growth has been the wrapper. Glassine and paper wrappers were replaced by poly bags. And the labels have been redesigned and upgraded with the assistance of a packing supplier. The Amana logo-type, a wagon wheel, long a hallmark of the Amana design, has been retained. However, it has been embellished with three and cour-color prinint. Over-all, the label tells the type of product, the price, information on ingredient contents, etc. — all in bright combinations of eye-appealing colors.

In Honolka's view, the poly bags have yielded several easy to identify benefits. They include outstanding visibility, an impression of cleanliness, and product protection. On this final point. Honolka feels the poly bag adds "days" to product freshness — a particularly important feature in the light of the extensive truck routes maintained.

Who buys Amana "home style" breads? In Honolka's view, "Certainly, there is no question of the appeal that seems principally to be to folks who have known "home-made" breads in their past. People with rural backgrounds or from recent European family stock are the most typical. This usually means the purchaser is older — perhaps 40 - 45. The exceptions are young people who have traveled outside the United States and who have discovered the pleasure of thc varicty brcads." "I'm confident," he concludes, "this share of the bread market can grow."

FAMILY MEMORIES

1983 Eulogy for John Honolka, Sr.
Given by Eva Honolka Newman

April 28, 1983
Moore Funeral Home Chapel
1219 N. Davis Dr
Arlington, TX 76012

JESUS TAUGHT US, THAT THE truth about each man lay in his spirit and not the physical world. Religions and temples are built my man, but Gods' temple is man, and wherever we are we are always in a place of worship. Life is the medium through which we seek to work out that purpose. When that purpose is fulfilled it is time for us to return home once again.

We are here today to say farewell to our beloved Father, Grandfather and Husband. We come with respect and admiration with gratitude in our hearts for his courageous leadership – for he was a pioneer in a difficult time and a difficult era – but nevertheless a pioneer to this great land called America.

He was a man of great physical strength, participating in competitive sports. He skied, loved hockey and soccer. Dad reveled in challenge and he challenged life.

John had great mental strength and abilities – that made him take the promise of opportunity that this country offered and became successful

in business. John worked hard and long hours, because work gave him dignity and he was a dignified man.

He loved this earth and all its natural beauty – and he took from this earth only what he needed – he never wasted. Dad was is quest of knowledge, to know the earth upon which he lived, and he expressed that love in the things he planted in his garden and the joy he expressed when he was surrounded by nature.

He was a giant in the community of businessmen. He marketed bread in several States from Iowa to Louisiana. It was his innovative approach which took the loaves out of the waxed paper and put them in the now familiar poly bags for greater convenience, freshness, and product visibility. John Honolka was not too lazy to bend over – he worked from 5:00 AM to 10:00 PM in his pursuit of happiness with hope to become a successful businessman.

He was a man – he had his faults – but he was humble and always responsible.

He was a good man and his goodness manifested itself in the love he had for his grandchildren, the little people on his Honolka clan. To them, I am sure he would have said this: "It is necessary to feel a sense of history."

You are part of what has come before and part of what is yet to come. Being this surrounded, you are not alone. Do not frivolously use the time that is yours to spend. Cherish it – that each day may bring new growth, insight, and awareness. Use this growth not selfishly, but rather in service. What may be in the future tide of time, never allow a day to pass that did not add to what was understood before.

John Honolka has gone home. His spirit lay down his body because it was finished with the work on this earth and John moves into the great expansion where he is part of the great universe, He is now with God in the endless time of eternity. As each of us – his 5 children – part of him continues, and it does make a difference that John Honolka lived, the world is a better place because he was in it.

For liberty he sacrificed a lot, but the divine gift of liberty is God's recognition of man's greatness and man's dignity. So, liberty be the sweetness of life and the power of growth. Under the spell of heavenly memorials John never had ceased to dream of liberty and aspire to its possession until it was caught up in his embrace, in a great and abiding nation.

I will miss my dad. I feel the pain and loneliness and life seems bleak and cold, but this is life, can you see. That dust to dust returned, but Godly souls and sweet memorials shall ever remain - I shall rise again.

2002 Julie Remembering Her Mother, Eva

The following is a letter that Julie Honolka Slaten submitted for a contest in "The Ladies Home Journal", January 2002.

My mother, Eva Honolka Newman, is an inspiration to me and to hundreds of others who have heard her story.

She was born in Czechoslovakia in 1937. Some of her earliest memories included the bombing of her city, the takeover of her fathers' business by the Communists. Her family tried to escape from the Communists but were captured and placed in a Hungarian prison. They escaped to Austria where they lived in displaced person camps for 2 ½ years.

After living in the camps for 2 ½ years her family came to America in April 1951. They settled in Iowa and had to start a new life with little money and no knowledge of the English language or American customs. Her father worked three jobs to support a family of seven.

My mother's parents felt strongly that she marries a Czech, so they arranged her marriage to Frank Newman, (the spelling of his name was changed from Neumann) a fellow Czech. At the age of 19 she was put on an airplane bound for Texas to marry him.

Frank Newman joined the U.S. Army of his adopted country. In 1970 he was killed in an airplane accident while serving his second tour of duty in Vietnam. My mother was left with three small children. (Mike 10, Julie 8, Chip 6) to raise.

She remarried in 1971 and from this marriage she bore two children. The first baby died from health complications when he was four days old. Her second child died at the age of three from a drowning accident. Not only had she lost two children from this marriage, but the deaths brought back the painful memories of her first child she had with my father. Her marriage to my stepfather was a difficult one and ended in divorce in 1978.

In 1980 her son Chip, at the age of 17, was killed in a car accident. I will never forget my mother's strong faith during that difficult time. She knew she had to be strong for my brother and me.

In 1977 she began giving speeches of her life experience from Czechoslovakia and the displaced persons camp. Over the past 25 years her speaking engagements have grown to include schools, churches, businesses, and many other organizations. She does not ask for money for her programs. She does it for the love of her adopted country, America. Through her speeches she conveys to her audiences just how precious freedom is. She likes to use the phrase "Freedom is not free." She values freedom and hopes her speeches have a positive impact on those who hear her.

Even though my mother has had a challenging life, she is a positive person that has a lot of faith. She has often told me without her faith she would have not survived the difficult times.

I am proud to call Eva Honolka Newman my mom and my hero.

2006 Eva Remembering her Mother, Jarmila

The clouds which darkened the earth in 1938 were clouds of the war and hate and evil. As children, we grasped and stumbled and the only emotion we had was fear. Fear of bombings, hunger, and all the atrocities that came with war. My Mother's protective faith guided us beyond darkness, of the difficult years, and we saw the sky of everlasting glory and the light of God.

In 1948 we escaped from the oppressive Communist government. As the night came, we left our homeland. The path was dark; we shook with cold and fear, but Mom drew us close and covered us with her coat. She was near and no harm could come to us.

The next day we walked far; we grew weary buy Mother cheered us on. "Be brave, soon we will be there". When we reached the boarders of two Countries, we realized we could not have done it without Mother. She taught us courage, fortitude in the face of harshness, strength to persevere, and faith in God. She taught us to stay frugal, not waste anything, and to share with others.

In 1951 Mom came to the United States of America with my Father and their five children. As refugee she dreamed of a life founded on new values, free of the myths of the Old World. The aspiration of a better life had an inner direction founded on the urge for the good and the true of this country, the United States of America. Mom studied the Constitution and the laws of the land. She cheered us on to learn the new English language so we could become good citizens. She was a Patriot.

The years passed; she grew old, but her children were tall and strong.

We walked with courage, faith, perseverance, and loyalty to our new country. Mother said "I know the end of my journey is better than the beginning, for my children can walk alone. Their children after them can enjoy freedom and with God's blessings."

I can no longer see my Mother, but she is always with me. She is a living presence. She lives in my laughter. She is crystallized in every teardrop. She is the smell of bleach in freshly laundered socks, she is the whisper of the leaves as I walk down the street.

My Mom is the map I follow with every step I take: Proverbs 31: 25–26 ESV. Strength and dignity are her clothing, and she laughs at the time to come. She opens her mouth with wisdom and the teaching of kindness is on her tongue.

2012 Remembering John and Jarmila Honolka

In 2012 Sharon Honolka asked the Grandchildren, and PC, to write a memory of their Grandparents, John and Jarmila Honolka. The following pages were a gift to their parents at Thanksgiving dinner.

Sgt. Phillip Carroll Callahan

Never met Jon Sr.

Jarmila would often tell me about her childhood. Most particularly when she was in school. For the first time in 400 years Czechoslovakia was a free country once again.

Jarmila went to her grave believing in these things. In 1938 Germany occupied Sudetenland and in March of 1939 remainder of the Czech lands.

They lived through the German occupation that lasted till 1945. Three brief years of freedom then communism took over in 1948.

After coming to the United States and becoming a citizen of the United States Jarmila Honolka always expressed a very deep and profound love for her Native Country.

David and Dan Grimm sons of Vlasta (Patricia)

Butchlee wore white uniforms and had a flat white hat. Had this big beer stein that mixed his concoctions and drank them.

He loved to watch 'Lawrence Welk." On Saturday he would come to take me, Mom and Dan to "Bishops" in Lindale

I remember fabulous vacations. I can remember one winter, they already left the Bakery and lived in Bettendorf, I remember it was cold and he was wrapped up with a blanket around his feet watching TV.

Butchlee, he had a nickname for me. I was called "Butchlee" and Dan was called "Spechle".

Kocoo, I loved everything she cooked. I loved watch her in the kitchen making chocolate rolls with cream filling & fruit fillings. I loved her peach dumplings. I liked Kocco's cooking.

Food was so much better back then.

I remember her playing songs on the harmonica and violin.

Kocoo loved to walk in the woods behind the bakery. I remember how talented she was with needlepoint.

She would often share stories about her Sister in Czechoslovakia.

She made a soup with liver balls that did not taste like liver. Everything she made was from scratch. So good.

With a limit income she maximized the dollar and made sure everyone had something.

On my Grandparents limited income I received $100. for graduation.

I was amazed that he knew his eyesight was failing and he continued to go ahead.

Ben Honolka, Son Tomas Honolka

Remembering Teetee, I recall him taking me to Randall Mill Park to play. One-time sticks with me, once I fell into the creek that runs through the park.

I remember I could not have been too old in age because when I fell in, I never hit the bottom of the creek. He just laughed. I also recall falling asleep listening to him watching wrestling on TV. He liked the Great Kabuki wrestler and chuckled every time he was on.

Remembering Coocoo, she made the best apple dumplings. It was a favorite of mine. The toast with pickle and boiled egg was always good as well.

She crocheted a lot and to this day we still have some Christmas tree ornaments she made.

Danny Honolka, Son of John Honolka, Jr.

I was 7 when Papaw passed and 11 when Mamaw passed so memories are a few because of how young I was.

I remember them babysitting me a lot while my parents were at work.

Eating (always) home cooked meals, going for walks, playing in the backyard (shirtless).

I would just walk around the yard mostly looking at the plants, flowers and walking down to the creek.

There was a tree swing that I liked as well. They loved being outdoors with me and I remember helping them water the plants.

Mamaw had a harmonica that she played in the house as I watched endless hours of Mr. Rogers and Sesame Street.

I would love to watch World Class Championship Wrestling with Papaw as he laughed hysterically at the wrestler's silly antics.

I believe that is what got me into watching it as well through my early teen years.

It was always beautiful over there and peaceful to me.

I love landscaping and having a great yard because of them today (and my father). Now that I wrote this, I really miss that.

Jack Honolka, Son of Don Honolka

My memories of my grandparents in the Amana bakery were Pindy working behind the desk and Kookoo in the kitchen and us running all over the bakery. It was a great place to explore.

When they moved to the Quad Cities, I remember Pindy taking us ice skating when it was dark, and he did not see well in the dark.

I think he wanted us to have fun. He called us the Pindy Boys.

I really do not remember too much, other than he was a workaholic.

Jim Honolka, Son of Don Honolka

To this day my Grandmother, Jarmila Honolka was one of the nicest people I have ever met.

I remember my Grandfather, John Sr. being a profoundly serious man and I feel I inherited that seriousness. He was serious about his work time. I am serious about my work time on the mountain skiing. My work time is also my playtime.

I believe every athletic ability I have been passed down to me from my Grandfather.

I wish I got to know them more.

Beau Honolka, Son of Tom Honolka

I was too young to remember Grandfather and Grandmother Honolka.
I am interested in reading what others have had to say.

Jon Honolka, III, Son of Don Honolka

When Sharon called Jon to see what he remembers, she was amazed.
He started to share to story from the 1960's and 70's. She just listened.

Iowa Times:

The Pindy Boys
No fingerprints on the equipment
His Father's, early morning routes then a move to Davenport

Texas Times:

Jon loved his Grandmothers Chicken and Dumplings
Their home was peaceful and had a warm feeling.
He remembers Grandfather watching Game and Sports Shows
Taking walks in the park.
She was always making things with her hands and needle and thread.
Then he said they moved to Ozark and found it was too hot, so they
    moved back to Texas.
He talked about when his Grandfather and Grandmother passed

Susie Honolka Missimo, Daughter of John Honolka, Jr.

When Sharon asked the Grandchildren to write a memory of their
Grandparents my first thought was, "Gosh I was so young when they
both passed away". My worry was that my memory would be limited.
However, the more I thought or went back to the past, I then realized
that the many little things they did for me had an impact/influence on
me today.

My Grandparents were nurturers, mentors, and role models:

1. Nurturers- I remember my grandmother always babysitting me when my parents needed help due to work, etc. I also remember my grandfather picking me up from elementary school after school. He would take me to their house and feed me a snack. I would then watch TV and take a nap until my parents came to pick me up. Both were always there to help. This alone aided in me learning later in life how supporting one another can make a difference and is important. It supports the saying It takes a village to raise a child. I believe this to be true.

2. My Grandparents were also mentors to me. I remember both my Grandparents being talented. My Grandma was a great cook. I remember liking most of the food she made. But especially the strudels she made- they were delicious. I also remember her liking cream cheese. She wanted to put it on all my toast with jelly. Let us just say I was too young to appreciate it then but now I love cream cheese on my toast. And furthermore, she hated all the pickles I would constantly eat. I did eat a lot of them so I guess now I can see why she worried.

   My Grandmother also loved crocheting and sewing many different things. I remember her crocheting a beautiful pink shawl that both my daughters had worn when they were babies. I remember how proud I was to tell people that my grandmother had made it. I also feel she would be proud to say that her great granddaughters were both able to wear it.

   I remember her crocheting Christmas ornaments to put on our tree. I thought these were so beautiful. She also made me a doll that looks like me when I was little- a little tom boyish looking girl with yellow yarn for my hair. I loved it, and still have it today.

   She was a great artist. I remember us drawing and coloring together, and her drawing me pictures. I asked her one day to draw me a princess. I remember taking it home and trying to copy it because I thought it was so good.

My Grandfather used to call me "Lady Fish". I loved this. He would come over to watch me swim sometimes. I loved to swim, could swim for hours, and would not get tired. He would laugh watching me swim, hence, the name "Lady Fish". I also loved it when he would come over to my house to babysit me and would bring chocolate candy bars. One had fruit and nuts in it, and the other was filled with caramel. I would sit and watch Benny Hill episodes with him and eat the candy bars. They were delicious, and I loved it. I would also get a kick out of hearing him laugh at Benny Hill.

Last, I remember both caring for their yard. They both loved plants and worked in the yard. I remember seeing both at different times watering the backyard. It is funny how most of these talents/skills are of interest to me today. I love to cook, I love drawing/art, painting, I love gardening, and God knows I love desserts and chocolate.

3. Role Models- Well this is a no brainer to me. Any Grandparent that would sacrifice their own lives, and give up everything they had built for freedom, and to provide a better lifelong term for their children and future Grandchildren speaks volumes about believing in your principles and fighting for what you believe is right.

Everything I have and enjoy today is essentially due in part to them. When I think of this, I am grateful, proud, and would say they are heroes because of this. I am honored to call them my grandparents.

Mike Newman son of Eva Honolka Newman

I have fond memories of my grandparents. I still see John in his white bakery clothes. I remember following him as he worked, always explaining why he did something or what made one dough different from another. His accent was awesome, the best I ever heard.

Jarmila worked magic creating masterpieces out of simple ingredients. Whether it was a meal or embroidery, she was talented. Sadly, though, she did not see it herself. She was remarkably well-informed and could discuss intelligently anything that was in the news.

I miss my Grandma and Grandpa. One of my big regrets in life is that I did not take the opportunity to learn more from them. But there are still all the wonderful memories.

Julie Newman Slaten, Daughter of Eva Honolka Newman

The first memory I have of my grandparents is when we lived in Columbus, Georgia during 1964 and 1965. I remember them coming to visit for Easter and helping us kids hunt for Easter eggs. I found it fascinating when they would talk in Czech to my parents and would wonder if they were, they are talking about us kids. I remember thinking they seemed so old.

One of the fondest memories I have of my grandparents occurred in the summer of 1970. 1970 was a very tough year for our family because our dad died in February of that year. To help us kids develop some good memories for that year my mom thought it would be a good idea for us to spend some time with our grandparents by ourselves. My mom put Mike, Chip, and I on a plane bound for Iowa to visit Grandma and Grandpa. They came to the airport to pick us up in a light blue sedan. What I found most interesting about the car was the plastic "bubble wrap" that covered the seats in the car. It would make a funny noise when you sat on it, but I thought it was cool.

I do not remember everything about the trip, but I do remember having a great time. Grandpa would take us to the bakery and show us how they made bread. I remember the huge vats of dough all over the bakery and the ovens full of baking bread. Oh, how I remember that wonderful smell of fresh baked bread. I honestly believe my love of bread (it is my favorite food) comes from my grandfather's talent of bread making. He would let us have some dough and we would play with that dough in the bakery for hours. And the best part is we would get to eat some of the bread.

I remember thinking the bakery was such a neat place. I loved the area they lived in above the bakery. There are several things I do remember about their living area. I remember the metal steps on the outside that led up to the kitchen, the huge room in the middle of the house where they had a picnic table for eating, the blacktop roof area, and how the bedrooms could each be entered from the big living area.

I also remember grandpa taking us to Marengo, Iowa. It was a quaint little town with a beautiful downtown square. I do not remember what we did there, but I am sure we had a good time.

Another particularly good memory I have of my grandfather, of course, involves bread. He would send us a big box full of a variety of breads he made in the bakery. I am not sure how often he sent the boxes to us, but I really enjoyed them when he sent them. My favorite item inside the boxes he sent was the butter horns. To this day I still remember the taste of them. Even though I was just a kid, when the bread arrived, I would eat a whole bag of butter horns in one sitting. They could not have lasted awfully long, and I do not remember if my brothers liked them has much as I did.

I do not remember the exact year my grandparents left the bakery, but I do remember feeling incredibly sad that there would be no more bread from grandpa. I do remember they moved to Ozark for approximately one year I believe in 1971 or 1972. The year they were in Ozark we had a record snowfall (it rarely snowed in Ozark) of eight inches. Grandpa thought it was so funny that people in Ozark were making such a big deal over this massive snowstorm. I remember my mom, grandma, and I went walking in the snow and had a great time. I loved living close to them for the first time in my life. They lived in a small three-bedroom house on Cherry Street. It was nice to be able to go over and visit them anytime we wanted because before we only got to see them once every two or three years. I do remember being sad when they moved to Texas.

One special thing I do remember about my grandmother was all the beautiful things she could make with her hands. My mom has many of her pillowcases and tablecloths that she embroidered by hand. And do not forget the cooking. I do not remember many of the things she could cook but I know she made wonderful dumplings, which, surprise, is another favorite food of mine. I really believe I could live off dumplings and butter horns, and my mom would agree.

I remember when both Grandma and Grandpa died. I wish that I had gotten to know them more and asked them about their lives before they came to the United States. I know they were highly intelligent and gifted people that had to overcome so many hardships along their journey of life. I am enormously proud to have come from such special people.

EVA'S SPEAKING ENGAGEMENTS AND MEDIA

1983 He Pursued Happiness with Hope

The American Consumer – The Consumer Benefit Association, Inc.
P. O. Box 4993, Montgomery, AL 36103-4993, 205-264-8672
3rd Quarter 1983 Issue
By: Gordon Tucker, Editorial Director

I NEVER KNEW JOHN HONOLKA personally.

I wish I had, for he was a giant in the community of businessmen, but before this story is done, we both will know him better and hopefully will be the better for the knowledge.

He was not a native-born American, but he taught all of us who are what our role as such should be. Entertain no doubt about it, he was American to the core. And here we speak in the connotation of the sense in which that word was originally applied.

Former Treasury Secretary Bill Simon must have been speaking of the exact opposite when he penned these words some two years ago: "We know about the rip-off artists in the welfare, food stamp and CETA programs, but I've concluded that certain businessmen aren't much better.

The breed that I am thinking about are worse, in fact, because they above all other citizens should appreciate and defend the values of free enterprise and self-reliance. Yet, all too often they seek bailouts, federal favors, or regulatory protection conferring competitive advantage.

John Honolka knew better. He would make no such requests and indulge in no such practices, because he of all people knew all too well that whenever government is structured and encouraged to play the role of "Helping Hand," then sooner or later it owns you.

This was the very thing from which he said boldly and successfully, though not without terrible cost, sought escape.

He had been the manager of a chocolate factory in his native Czechoslovakia before and during WWII, but there was always the gnawing desire to enter business for himself – to become an owner in his own right.

The ambition was realized in 1945 at the close of the war when he established Koruna Fancy Pastries. In mere months, his success was ensured. In less than three years the business was booming. He had become what he had always wanted to be - a man with an idea that had found its time and was now a tangible, working reality that provided jobs for his assistants, delectable treats for his customers, and the good things of life for his family.

The fundamental traits of willingness to take a risk, personal initiative, self-reliance, and hard work had paid off.

But, hadn't you heard, John Honolka? These things are discouraged when applied to your own interests – especially business interests – in those nations whose governments tended towards a collective bent, and John, one day when you weren't looking your elected representatives in Parliament were shouted down and displaced by a minority of collectives of the worst stripe, and your government was taken over by the communists.

Suddenly, without your hardly realizing it, black and white, night and day, dark was light, and all your good traits were just so many dead weights for now, John Honolka, you were a capitalist in a Communist land. The worst label with which you could be tagged.

Overnight you were in a different atmosphere – Friends became distrustful of friends, brothers turned against brothers, and neighbors against neighbors. Even the children were drawn into the controversy. Incredible, you may have though. John, until the incident of your little daughter, Eva brought it straight home to you.

As children do at times, they will be children in a spate of name-calling. And this is what little Eva did – during an exchange with a neighbor-child one day she resorted to the most demeaning title her little thought process – could conjure up – "You – You communist, You.

To the utter astonishment within mere hours John Honolka was taken into custody for interrogation. Indoctrinating his children against communism and its benefits.

Though released after a warning against teaching such attitudes to his offspring, doubtless he was not only astonished, but shaken as well. Bear in mind this was in Czechoslovakia which had been the Central European Showcase on Democracy between World Wars. Now his nation was in the throes of a totalitarian take-over who instrument of control was terror.

It was within the general period of 1948 that John fell victim to an extended illness brought on by a chronic throat infection which in turn led to a three week stay in the hospital and accompanying absence from his business.

He returned to a far different world.

While no money had exchanged hands, yet a man was seated at his desk who informed him that his business had been nationalized and now belonged to the state.

"No man should own so much, or control this many workers," he was told. "This is permitted only to the state."

One wonders if it dawned on John Honolka that moment the fallacy that is contained in such assertion. Where on earth did mankind gets the mistaken notion that a so-called "crime" perpetrated by an individual is any less a criminal act when committed by government?

Indeed, this is the measure by which all outrages against individual liberty and abuses of power by government should be defined.

As Frederic Bastial so aptly put it: "See if this act (of government) benefits one citizen (group of citizens or businesses) at the expense of another (citizen, group of citizens or business) by doing what the benefited citizen himself cannot do without committing a crime.

This is the standard which must be applied to all official acts affecting life, liberty, and property if government is to be kept in its proper place and perform its rightful role, that of preventing injustice from overtaking even one citizen that another or others might be enriched.

It is, of course, the antithesis of this philosophy which confiscated John Honolka's pastry business and made him an "enemy of the people".

He could of course redeem himself, he was told, if he chose to lend his status (of which he had his share) in the community to the Party (communist) by joining up and working in the interest of its aims and goals, which in their words was to "establish a great new society in the land."

How he must have been applauded in later years after he had reached these shores to hear these same words (Great Society) spoken in all seriousness by an American President as descriptive of the goal to which his administration aspired.

We forget: Government is not omnipotent; only God is.

"Just join us," the Communists cooed "and we will work together for the betterment of all".

They even offered to let him stay on with the business as its manager. How generous. To remain a manager of what was once his own imagination and initiative – how generous, indeed.

He rejected their sleazy bribe hands down, and in the act became a marked man. This was on a Saturday.

It has been said that the "mills of the gods grind slowly."

Not so, the machinery of Atheistic Marxism. The following day (Sunday) he took his family for a walk in the park and there in their presence was arrested for "illegal activities against his government, and not cooperating in the best interests of society and the state".

His real "crime" of course, was that he was simply a capitalist by philosophy and practice – a Naboth who only wanted his vineyard that which was his own.

The family was sent home, but the next day they took the mother as well – questioning her feelings about the government and explored the general status of her attitude towards the new regime – was informed that John Honolka would be kept in custody and made to labor in the coal mines until he was "re-educated."

In jail for two weeks in his hometown he was indeed, indoctrinated daily; but then a problem came up at the business as in many instances when a plant is nationalized and placed in the hands of incompetents.

John would be released if he would assist in the alleviation of the problem.

Oh. "all-knowing" torturers, are you not aware that this John Honolka whom you made your victim was also a man, even as each of you, with intelligence, the faculty to observe, to know, to think, to plan and to judge for himself; else why did you call him back to his post?

He bowed at their shrine only long enough to escape it. With the help of the underground, he made his way to Vienna only to turn back to rescue his family, but this time he was arrested just before getting to the border of Austria and the family was split up for 9 months.

During this period, he was in three months of hard labor – more accurately, hard abuse – at the hands of the Communist attempt to "re-educate" him – strung up by his wrists, beaten with heavy leather straps until his back was scarred for life – a mute testimony to one man's conviction that human dignity is preserved only if the spirit is permitted to run free.

He was told oh so reasonably, John Honolka we must stunt individual liberty and personal development.

John might have added, it dehumanizes and enslaves, and therefore our founding fathers knew that it is government which must be restrained and kept within bounds-not bodies and souls which should be manhandled.

John Honolka's spirit remained free and after nine months his body was free also having made another escape and with the aid of the American Red Cross was reunited with his family – he'd had lost track of them completely – in the French Sector of Austria, the city of Salzburg to be exact.

The ordeal and accompanying deprivations (and there were many for the Honolka Family as it waited out three long years in displaced persons camps and their agonizingly slow success in finally being accepted by a sympathetic country is a story but suffice it to say that they did make it out of Europe – originally slated to go to New Zealand, but at the last minute switched to America – and on to a new life.

"A worthy man for acceptance into the American Community," it was said of John Honolka; and this proved to be the case when he made a successful life here for himself and family – again in the business be knew best – baking.

In fact, he marketed the "staff of life" (bread) in several states, from Iowa (where he settled) to Louisiana. It was his innovative approach which took the loaves out of waxed paper and put them in the now familiar poly bags for greater convenience, freshness, and product visibility.

John Honolka lived 32 years to the day after having arrived in New Orleans on 26 April 1951.

America is the better for that 32 years, for he lived as he believed: that there is gold in the streets of America if you are not too lazy to bend over and pick it up. It lies in the promise that America offers to work as a free man and pursue happiness with hope.

John Honolka was not too lazy to bend over. in fact, during his first four years in America with no proof of his education and work background he had to take what came: two jobs as a janitor, one job as a butcher and one job as a supermarket clerk in the produce department. He performed all four jobs every day, six days per week, beginning at 5:00 a.m. until 10:00 p.m. at night but his pursuit of happiness with hope paid off: he once again became a successful businessman.

What lesson does John Honolka hold for the average American businessman?

His daughter Eva and I chatted about it one night recently and we came to the approximate conclusion.

The lesson lies in recognizing the value of a personal incentive that will reach out and take hold of the opportunities provided by Freedom as we have known it in America; but that Freedom must be guarded. You do not take it for granted. Therefore, you do not, you must not ignore those indiscretions of government which would immobilize the opportunities it provides.

A wayward government must be kicked in line more swiftly than a wayward person who tries to rob you of your liberty, for unlike John Honolka, you may not get a second chance.

I never met John Honolka. I wish I had.

1986 Czech Refugee Tells of Early Escape

The Army Flier – Fort Rucker, Alabama
By: Marion Jones, Friday, January 19th

Faces on passports tell the story of her early life – from a drawn-faced waif whose eyes reflected some of the horror she had seen as a refugee, to that of a healthy child returning in a displaced persons camp after a recuperative stay in Switzerland and finally to that passport photo where she posed with family as they embarked on a new life in the United States.

To see the blue-eyed sparkling beauty of Mrs. Frank Newman one would never know of the personal drama that has taken place in her life – tales of escape, capture and re-escape.

Eva Newman met her future husband Major Frank Newman, commanding officer of the Foreign Military Training Division, when they were both refugees, living in displaced persons camps in Germany. They had both escaped from Czechoslovakia after the Communists took over following World War II.

Eva's father, a Czech businessman was arrested by the Communists who took over his business. Through contacts with the underground, he managed a hair-raising escape for his family into Austria where he joined them later after making the same miraculous escape.

Major Newman was a law student in Czechoslovakia when the Communist showed loomed in his country. Like students everywhere he exercised his right to protest the new regime and was forced to leave.

Decent, responsible men were needed to become the leaders of the displaced persons camps which were springing up all over Germany. Frank Newman became the leader of me in one of these camps. Eva's father was the leader of another. She was only 12 years old at the time of their first meeting.

After many frustrations, her father was able to secure clearance for the family's immigration to the United States. The family did not find life to be all milk and honey after their arrival. The father, though well educated, had trouble finding gainful employment. Eva worked when she was 14 as a maid for $1 per day. The whole family worked and worked hard to gain a foothold in their newly adopted land. Her father's saying. "Courage, what it takes? Courage what I got" became a family motto.

The family did not hear again from their friend in Germany until one day a friend mentioned that "Frank Newman if going to OCS now." Eva's father wrote and asked him to spend Christmas with the family. By this time Eva was a teen-ager, a cheerleader, addicted to hamburgers three times a day. Frank Newman was an officer candidate – cool, calm, and collected. It was love at first sight for him, but she needed some extra time to consider the proposal of marriage which was soon forthcoming.

They were married in Texas where Major Newman was undergoing flight training. She had the long traditional white wedding gown, he bought the wedding bouquet to match the blossom detail of the gown's lace, a reception was held in the officer's club and the happy couple ate sardines for their wedding dinner. Frank Newman was not the first nor the last second lieutenant to overextend himself.

Eva Newman hates to hear people say that Americans are spoiled. "You made it good for yourself. Too many nations criticize nowadays," she states.

Now that all three of her children are in school Mrs. Newman has the mornings to herself but she is not wasting them by late sleeping, bridge, and coffee with the girls. She is taking piano lessons from a lady in Ozark – something she has yearned to do for many years. Art lessons are being planned for the near future.

Frank and Eva Newman are naturals in his position with the Foreign Military Training Division. They understand the problems of newcomers to a strange land. When foreign students are invited to her home for dinner Mrs. Newman takes time beforehand to learn their backgrounds and religion, taboos so that she may plan her meals accordingly.

When asked about Czech cooking Mrs. Newman stated that dumplings, sour kraut, and pork roast are the equivalent of potatoes, salad, and steak in the United States. She makes a delicious pastry called Jahodove Rezy.

Strawberry Squares
4 eggs separated.
1 cup sugar
¾ cup flour
½ teaspoon of salt
2 teaspoons of lemon juice
1 teaspoon lemon rind

Beat yolks with sugar until lemon colored and very fluffy. Add lemon juice. Fold in flour alternately with stiffly beaten egg whites. Add lemon rind last. Pour into well-greased and floured pan. Bake at 350 degrees until brown, about 25 minutes. When cool cut in half and spread with butter rum filling

Butter Rum Filling
1 stick margarine
1 ½ cups confectioners' sugar
1 egg yolk
1 teaspoon rum

Beat well about 5 minutes. Spread over one of the cake halves and put halved strawberries on top. Place the other cake half on top and spread the remainder of the icing on top and decorate with whole strawberries. Cut in squares and refrigerate till served. Other fruits may be used besides strawberries.

1989 With Great Pride Native of Czechoslovakia

Tells of Her Family's Struggle for Freedom
The Alabama Journal, Montgomery, AL
Monday, July 10, 1989
By Nick Lackeos

Sitting in the living room of her Montgomery home on a recent rainy afternoon, Eva Honolka Newman reflected on her pride in America.

Even before she spoke, that pride was evident. The table next to the easy chair where Mrs. Newman sat featured a small photograph of the Statue of Liberty. At the front of home, just off the Atlanta Highway, a large flag rippled in the breeze.

"I think you reach a stage in your life when you're in love with something greater than what you are." she spoke. "And in my case, it's the love of my country – the United States.

During a time, some Americans are burning the flag to protest, Mrs. Newman is doing all she can to spread a feeling of patriotism, by speaking to various civic clubs and other organizations. After all, she believes, it is the least she can do for a country that allows her such freedom.

"It's paying something back to America." Said Mrs. Newman, a native of Czechoslovakia who immigrated with her family to the United States at the age 15 in the early 1950s. "I love this country."

Mrs. Newman has been involved in public speaking since an early age. She first told of her family's history and their arrival in the United States during a school assembly in Iowa when she was 17. And over the years as a military wife, traveling throughout the nation and to Europe, she told her story whenever she was asked.

Born in Trutnov, Czechoslovakia in 1937, Mrs. Newman came into the world about the same time the German troops moved into the mountains of her native country. By the time she was is elementary school, German planes were bombing the cities.

"I started to school in 1943" She said. "I remember the bombings and the food lines and the terror – of occupation by another nation over you.

"I could hear the bombs dropping, and I remember the schoolhouse shaking. You were rushed down into the school basement. When the bombs stopped and you came up from the basement, you did not know if your house was still standing.

"you don't forget something like that. I think fear is something we seldom forget."

After the war, Mrs. Newman's father, a businessman who detested communism, devised a plan to get away from Soviet jurisdiction. He took his wife, two daughters and three sons and left Czechoslovakia.

"We were caught in Hungary in 1948 and put in a displaced persons camp," all except Mrs. Newman's father, she said. He was sent to a separate camp and tortured by communist authorities who were trying to persuade him to accept communism, she said.

For six months, Mrs. Newman's family was detained at Tolinshaus, a prison in Budapest, Hungry. The conditions were very crude, and the people were treated in a dehumanizing manner, she said.

"I was 11 years old, and we were in a huge room with 500 women and children." She spoke.

Each prisoner's daily rations consisted of a red and green pepper and some mush that resembled cream of wheat.

"Babies died there of malnutrition," she said. "When babies died, the guards would come and pick up their little bodies. They would put them in a paper sack and take them away. It was a nightmare. My little brother, Tomas (Tom) was 18 months old and had malnutrition. The peppers were feeding us were eating his stomach up.

The surroundings were filthy and lacked toilet facilities.

"I remember we were sitting there on the straw and my mother was picking fleas and ticks out of my little brother's hair," she said.

Mrs. Newman's mother knew she had to get her family out of the camp. Finally, she seized the opportunity to escape when, for unknown reasons, the guard at the front desk left his post.

"Mother took a chance and walked out of the prison with us," she said.

Although they were weak from so little food and had no money, the family walked to a railroad depot and boarded a train. At one point, it looked as if they might have to return to the camp when Mrs. Newman's mother exchanged words with two guards – one considerably older than the other.

"I remember my mother told them: In the name of God and these little children, don't send me back," she said. "The old man looked at the young man and said: "I do not see anything, do you?"

They let us stay on the train. We passed on into Vienna."

The family stayed in a refugee camp in Vienna, which was in a Russian zone, for two days. But, Mrs. Newman's mother, discovered that they would be sent back to Czechoslovakia by Soviet authorities if they could not reach the refugee camp in the French zone in Salzburg, took advantage of the lax supervision in the camp and took her children and left.

"I was 12, and I remember a farmer let us hide in his hay wagon," Mrs. Newman said. "He had a huge haystack on his wagon and something like an igloo in the middle of the hay. We hid in there. He took us to Salzburg, and he was stopped by the Russians along the way.

"They took pitchforks and stuck them in the hay. I remember a pitchfork coming so close to my head. I had nightmares about that for a long time.

Eventually the family made it to the Salzburg camp. In the meantime, her father had escaped from the prison camp where he was being held.

"My father got to Vienna and went to the American Red Cross" to locate his family, she said. "Within three weeks, the Red Cross located us and gave my father money. That's when we became a family again."

The family was forced to remain in camps for three more years before other arrangements could be made. Finally, giving up on hopes to go to the United States, they were set to board a ship for New Zealand where they had been accepted by the immigration authorities.

We desperately wanted to immigrate to the United States, Mrs. Newman Said. "But the American immigration authorities would do a two-year investigation into your background, checking things like your medical history. If your grandfather had tuberculosis, for example, they would refuse you for fear you might be carrying the disease."

But a day or so before they were to sail to New Zealand, they were notified that they had received permission to go to the United States. After arriving in New Orleans, the family set out for Iowa.

In those post-war years, a sponsor from the United States paid passage for a family to immigrate to the United States and the family paid the sponsor back. For their first eight months on American soil, Mrs. Newman's family farmed 500 acres of land to pay their debt.

The family continued to live in Cedar Rapids for about three years before moving to Amana, Iowa, which was made up mostly of a settlement of German Americans, she said. A group of businessmen there, "took a chance on my father" and signed for his bank loan that he used to start his own business.

"He opened a bakery, the Amana Society Bakery, and we marketed bread over five states," she said. "He developed the plastic bag for bred, because bred was in wax paper then, and the wax paper would crack when you froze the bread for shipment".

In 1956, after her graduation from Amana High School, Mrs. Newman was offered a scholarship to study art at the Art Institute in Chicago. However, her father refused to let her go to the city.

My father said, "A young woman of 19, living by herself in Chicago, a city full of Mafia? Never." she said.

Besides, Mrs. Newman said, her future had already been determined for her. Shortly after her graduation, she was flown to Austin, Texas, to meet the man her father had arranged for her to marry. Her husband to be was a native Czech her father has met in a displaced person's camp, and the young man, Frantisek Neuman (later changed to Frank Newman) was a leader among the prisoners.

The young man had been a college preparatory student in Prague during the war but was forced into a Nazi slave labor group in 1945, she said. After the war, he was accepted in 1946 as a law student at Charles University, the oldest university in Central Europe.

But while he was a law student, Newman became interested in politics and joined with other students in protesting the new Czechoslovakian government that was controlled by the Soviet communists. He fled the secret police in 1948 but was captured in 1949.

He then escaped and made his way to Vienna and then to French occupied Germany where he was placed in Bad Wurzbach, a displaced person's camp. While there in 1952 he enlisted in the United States Army under the Lodge Act of 1952 and later underwent training to become an officer.

1991 Asian Fruit Tree A Living Legacy from Dad

The Montgomery Weekly Advertiser
October 19, 1991
By: Jennifer A. Walker, Advertiser Staff Writer

Eva Honolka Newman is banana about elephant ears and banana plants. She has dozens of them lining her yard. But, to her, the 25 feet tall banana trees and elephant ears as big as car hoods are more than a hobby. They are a living memorial to the husband she lost in Vietnam.

Ms. Newman's husband, LTC Frank Charles Newman, left their three children and their home in Ozark, AL to be an army pilot during the Vietnam War.

"My boys were always asking me, "What's it like where Daddy is?" she said. "I'd tell them. "it's a jungle with lots of green."

But Ms. Newman wanted to give her children a better idea of what the jungle was like. So, she encouraged her husband to smuggle a banana plant bulb from Vietnam.

When her husband was given leave, Ms. Newman met him in Hawaii and got the "illegally" imported Vietnam banana plant. And, while in Hawaii, she also bought back an elephant ear plant.

Once back in Ozark, Alabama, Ms. Newman put the fist sized banana bulb in a pot in her home.

That March, Mr. Newman was expected to return home from the war. Five days before his return, he was killed in action.

That spring, Ms. Newman decided to plant the last gift from her husband.

"One day I looked out there and saw these two leaves growing out and lo and behold...." She said. Her plant had begun to grow and grow

until fall, when the plant soared to more than 30 feet and was so wide, her arms could not reach around it.

Everyone in the small town of Ozark, AL knew about Ms. Newman, "They'd say. "Eva's gone bananas with this banana plants," she said.

She even "slipped a banana leaf into the church," one day when the townspeople were showing off their large fruit and vegetables, "Everyone said, "What's that", and I said. "It's my harvest."

Aside from the interest it created in other people, the towering plants, nested next to the gigantic elephant ears, were ideal for the children, who were than able to get a taste of the jungle and their father.

"My children have not stopped looking for that missing link – their father." She said. "The plant is sort of like a living memorial, if you know what I mean."

Every fall, the towering stalks of the banana tree are cur down to about 1 to 2 feet and hauled away. The stump is then fertilized as it waits through the summer until spring when temperatures rise to the 80's or 90's. The plant spurts over the roof in the six months of tropical like weather.

Since then, Ms. Newman has moved to Montgomery and planted her banana plants and elephant ears in her yard. She has given about 65 banana plants to friends and relatives in Alabama, Georgia, Texas, and Kansas. And she never charges a cent.

"I would no more sell them than the man on the moon." She said. "They were given to me to pass along."

During February of 2020 Don and Sharon made a trip to Ozark, AL. They met, Mr. Tom Wyse current owner of the Newman residence. Eva's handwriting was easily viewed in the corner of the driveway. Mr. Wyse says "People stop all the time and ask about the banana trees and elephant ears. We could easily view Eva's plantings have survived over 50 years and continue to flourish.

1992 I Feel Like the Lord Gave Me A Mission

1992 Montgomery Advertiser
By: Roxanne Barnes and Frank Mastin, Jr.

Let it be said Eva Newman loves God, country, and people in general. A State Employee and Capital Receptionist. Mrs. Newman likens herself and the five others to salesmen, whether on duty at the State Capitol or at the First White House of the Confederacy.

"We are like salesmen who are selling that state of Alabama to the public," she said, adding, "We believe in our product."

Although Mrs. Newman spends a lot of time conducting tours and giving directions, her duties do not end there.

"On one hand," she said, "we have information, and on the other hand is the relational element (sic). Both of those must come together to make an impact of people," she said. "People respond best when we relate information that is meaningful. It's our job as receptionists and guides to make it easy on our listeners," she said.

"How do you know what people want?" Mrs. Newman asked, rhetorically, "The answer is simple," she said, "It has nothing to do with the subject or how articulate we are. It has everything to do with people."

Mrs. Newman philosophized that every person wants attention and that she, as a receptionist, demonstrates that she is paying attention to her public by recognizing them and what is important to them.

"I know of no better way to relate to the public than by bringing them a caring attitude," Mrs. Newman said. "An attitude shows in our posture, facial expression, tone of voice. In all of these we communicate to our listeners, "I recognize your presence and your importance."

Mrs. Newman's philosophy is illustrated in an incident that occurred one day during a tour for senior citizens. The bus driver had a heart attack, Mrs. Newman said. She said that after they called paramedics, they were faced with keeping down the anxiety level of a large group of people. "We shared cookies, coffee and tea with them," she recalled. "it's important to have compassion for their situation."

She said the group was there for three or four hours before they were picked up by another bus.

"The job drains you, but it's rewarding, because you are selling your state." Mrs. Newman said. She said because you need to be physically fit to do what she does, she works out at a local gymnasium. She also gets somewhat of a workout while conducting tours of the Capitol. She routinely avoids the elevator and walks the three flights of stairs at the Capitol because visitors frequently take the stairs, she said. Born in Czechoslovakia in 1937, Mrs. Newman's family came to the United Sates as immigrants in 1951. She is a military widow and had six children. She has out-lived four of her five sons. Her two remaining children are Michael David, 33, an electrical engineer in Marietta, Ga., and Julie Ann, 31, who is in Human Resources with Protective Life Insurance Co. in Birmingham.

Mrs. Newman attended Amana High School in Iowa. Additionally, she has taken independent courses in human relations and human behavior, because it is just something she is interested in, she said, adding "I think the human being is the greatest thing ever created."

In addition to her workouts at the gym, she said, "I love bowling, jogging, and music," She also likes to play the piano and loves gardening. She likes to grow banana plants that her late husband gave her in Hawaii when he was on military leave from Vietnam, she said. The banana plants, she said, are her legacy to Vietnam veterans. She will provide a banana plant to "anybody who wants one gets one." she said.

Mrs. Newman also does personal testimonials to high schools, civic and church groups, and the boy scouts.

"She visited my Kiwanis club and held the group spellbound throughout the period she talked, mostly about her own life's tragedies and triumphs," said Frank Mastin, Jr., State Employee News editor & publisher. Mr. Mastin is a member of the Good Morning Kiwanis Club in Montgomery.

A State Employee for 10 years, Mrs. Newman said she has never taken a vacation. She has not, she said, because she has devoted all her time to her job and speaking engagements.

"I feel like the Lord gave me a mission, and that is to go and tell my story."

1992 Czech Native Shows Love for America

The Montgomery Advertiser – July 15, 1992
Around "N" About by Tom Conner

Probably nobody in Montgomery gets as deeply and emotionally involved with being an American as Eva Newman, especially on special occasions like the Fourth of July.

Eva is on the governor's staff and works as a Capital receptionist an as a Hostess at the first White House of the Confederacy. But, otherwise, her story is unique.

She was born Eva Honolka in Trutnov, Czechoslovakia, and believes in the principles of freedom and democracy in ways only those who live without them can understand. Her earliest memories include the devastation and capitulation of her native land to the Nazis, the bombing, food lines and the oppressive occupation by Hitler's forces and later Stalin's Soviet regime

"During the war, I would hear bombs fall, and I remember our school shaking. We rushed to the basement and wondered when we came out if anything was left. People don't forget that kind of fear I know I never will," she said.

Trying to escape from the Communist after the war, Eva's family was captured, then separated from her father when they were detained in different Hungarian prison camps. Miraculously, they all escaped to Vienna, where they were reunited with their father by the Red Cross. Her family finally received word that they had a U.S. sponsor and came to the United States. Eva married Frank Newman, a Czech native who had met her father in a displaced person's camp. Mr. Honolka arrange the marriage his daughter, Eva.

Eva lost her first child but later had five others, four sons and a daughter. Her husband was killed in a 1970 plane crash in Vietnam, only a few days before his second tour ended. Her son Chip was killed at the age of 17 by a drunken driver in an automobile accident.

But with all this tragedy and difficulty, Eva Newman is undaunted, sharing her life and her belief in America with people everywhere.

Everybody who hears her story is mesmerized by this inspiring woman. And Mrs. Newman tells the story with the gusto of the true Patriot that she is to audiences everywhere.

John Rosenblatt, a visiting associate professor at Auburn University perhaps some set up the best: "Your story moved each one of us and your pride in being an American citizen came out loud and clear. I think you should make an appearance in each high school in the entire state of Alabama and wherever else that is possible. Many members of the Armed Forces could improve their fighting spirit after being motivated by your most outstanding presentation."

Old King Solomon would have approved of Mrs. Newman. In his infinite wisdom, he concluded "Who can find a virtuous woman? For her price is far above rubies."

1993 Flag Day Is Memorial to One Montgomerian

East Montgomery Weekly, June 9, 1993
By: Kareem Crayton

"Everyone celebrates the 4th of July, but how many people celebrate Flag Day," asked a stately even Neuman, clothing red, white and blue period just as every American has a special reason to observe the occasion, so does she.

Miss Newman born into Trutnov, Czechoslovakia in 1937. She recalled the stages of the German takeover of her country during the earlier years of her life; "I remembered the bombings, the food lines and the terror of it all."

Her family endured both the Nazi occupation during World War II and the communist takeover that followed my father finally decided that we had to escape from the persecution Mrs. Newman said her family then began a long, dangerous passage out of the communist Europe. Miss Newman recalled many times when soldiers attempted to prevent her family from leaving after being displaced in several camps for almost four years, her family received permission to enter the United States.

"We were refugees more than we were immigrants" Mrs. Newman said. "Her father really detested the politics of the Communists and so we had to get out."

So, at the age of 16, Mrs. Newman's family made America their new home.

The family settled in Iowa, where Mrs. Newman entered school. Despite her age, she was placed in a fourth-grade class. Moving to such a new place is not easy, but the humiliation of going into a class with elementary students was worse." Mrs. Newman said. Nevertheless, Mrs. Newman understood the importance of starting school at that level. "I had to learn the language and the way of life here." she added.

"Just being welcomed into a country of freedom and liberty to me was more than I could have hoped for" said Mrs. Newman. "We came here with nothing and we were able to start a life."

After establishing his small business Mrs. Newman's father arranged for her to be married to a young soldier in Austin, TX. "We lived in America, but our foundation was still European", Mrs. Newman explained. The young serviceman, Frank Newman, had met her father in one of the Czechoslovakian displacement camps. Although he was Czech, he had joined the United States army while he was in Germany, she said. The two married on July 7, 1956 in Texas.

"Our marriage was quite fitting for such a patriotic day," Mrs. Newman said. "Even though we didn't know each other first, we slowly began to love each other," she added.

Because the Newman's were a military family, they lived in several different states. "We started in Austin and ended up in Boston," Mrs. Newman said. The family eventually included three children: Julie Anne, Chip, and Michael who was born on Flag Day. In the 1960s, the Newman's finally made their way to Ozark, near Fort Rucker. By then, Mrs. Newman's husband had attained the rank of LTC in the army. "Moving up from a foot soldier to an officer in the military was very rare for an immigrant," she said.

LTC Newman left the family to serve his country in Vietnam. Just before Frank's second tour of duty was over, we met for a few days in Hawaii, recalled Mrs. Newman. That was the last time I saw him.

LTC Newman was killed in combat only five days before he was to return home. Despite the hardship that Mrs. Newman suffered, she concentrated on the contribution of her husband. "He wanted to give back to the country that helped him," she said.

Mrs. Newman also had to endure the pain of losing her son, Chip, who died on Flag Day. "The last chore that Chip did at home was hang out the American Flag like he always did." Mrs. Newman said.

Despite the sadness connected with the day, Mrs. Newman has maintained her regard for Flag Day. "My pride for the stars and stripes just goes deeper and deeper, "she said.

Lecturing at local schools and civic organizations Mrs. Newman has committed herself to spreading ideas about patriotism. "Americans just don't have much pride in their country as they used to," she said. "Patriotism is the very heart and soul of an individual and a country."

Her lectures include her life story an experience with the American dream. "By the time I'm done I have the audience is full attention," she said.

"At baseball games when the national anthem is played people just go and buy food," Mrs. Newman said. "We ought to take more pride in America."

Although she admits that her story is an American dream, Mrs. Newman politically shies away from taking credit for the accomplishment. "What I have done is what everyone can do. That is the beauty of the United States," she said.

Mrs. Newman mentioned that her two other children both attended college and both have successful jobs. "The promise of opportunity that America offered me is fulfilled through my children," she said.

In Mrs. Newman's hands was the same flag the military gave her at her husband's funeral. "What we are celebrating is more than just the flag," Mrs. Newman said, clutching the tightly folded cloth of white stars and red stripes. "It is the symbol of what we are as individuals and as a country."

1994 Volunteer Winners Named

The Montgomery Weekly Advertiser
Friday, April 22, 1994

Montgomery volunteers received a community thank-you Thursday during the 20th annual Volunteer of the Year awards.

Fifty-six individuals and groups were nominated for the awards presented by The Volunteer and Information Center Inc. and The Montgomery Advertiser.

Eva Honolka Newman received the Sustained Superior Performance Award, the highest award given.

The naturalized American citizen has launched her own crusade to sell America, traveling the country telling her story of escape from her native Czechoslovakia and lauding the country that adopted her and her family.

Her volunteer efforts include sponsorship of international officers stationed at Maxwell Air Force Base, Girls State, Boys State, and the Hugh O'Brien Foundation.

1994 Ozark Woman Celebrates Freedom

Remembers Refuge from Communism
Refugee Embraces American Freedoms
The Southern Star, Ozark, AL
Wednesday, March 16, 1994
By: Rhonda Pines and Frank C. Williams, Staff Writers

A blond-haired, blue-eyed Czechoslovakia girl was stunned by what her early years had become; her father's arrest by Soviets, escapes from Hungarian prisons, a stay in German displacement camps, and refuge to Iowa where her impoverished family farmed the land.

That girl is now Eva Newman, a 50-year-old Ozark woman, one of about 15 people who gathered at the steps of the state capitol Friday to remember those who have suffered under communism.

Saturday was the 70th anniversary of the Bolshevik Revolution, which overthrew the Russian government for a communist society.

"For the Soviet Union, this is a celebration of conquest," said Earl Howard, state president of the American Freedom Coalition. "For those living under the rule, however, it is a day of mourning. Some mourn family members who have been jailed for political purposes, others mourn for those tortured and murdered at the blood-soaked hands of communist oppression."

During the noon ceremony, the group lighted red candles and displayed a 20-foot white banner bearing the names of countries and the day each came under communist rule. Several people present came from those countries, such as Hungry, Poland and Nicaragua. The program which included accounts of persecution, ended with the release of several dozen black balloons.

Newman, a receptionist at the First White House of the Confederacy, cherishes her rights in the United States, including the free enterprise system.

That ideal meant imprisonment and brutal beatings for her father after Czechoslovakia fell under communist rule.

John Honolka was a baker – until the day he arrived home to find his business destroyed because he employed too many people.

To Honolka, it was ambition. To the Soviets, it was capitalism, and he was arrested.

The family fled in 1948 but ended up in a Hungarian prison. Eva was 12.

Her father, a popular hockey and soccer league player, defied many communist ideologies. And when he consistently refused to adopt them, he was chained to the wall, his back stripped and beaten.

"My father died four years ago and to the day of his death, he had strap marks where the skin had been taken off," Newman said.

While in prison, her daily diet was two peppers – a green one and a red one, she said.

Malnutrition was commonplace, as were cries of sickly hungry babies and the tears of mothers who watched their dead infants carried away in brown paper bags, she said.

"The waiting and the screaming stays with me to this day," she said. "I don't think you ever forget. I don't think you can at that age."

After escaping from prison, the Honolkas lived in a German displacement camp for three years.

"We went to the community kitchen with our little pans," she said. They'd slop a ladle of something in it."

After standing in line for noodles, she once received worms.

"I told my mom I couldn't eat it," she said. "She told me it was 'the only meat you are going to get."

Since moving to the United States in 1951, Newman has passionately embraced the liberties of a free society. She pleaded that others do not take them for granted.

"The memory of this nation revolves around its brave and its heroes." She said, "who knew it's better to die fighting on one's feet than to live as slaves on one's knees."

1994 Immigrant Given Americanism Award

Eva Newman one of only handful in DAR's
history to be so recognized
The Montgomery On the Go, March 10, 1994
By: Special to The Independent

Eva Honolka Newman of Montgomery has been selected as the recipient of the prestigious "Americanism Award" by the Daughter of the American Revolution (DAR).

Newman was honored, along with recipients of other awards, at a special awards luncheon today.

The awards presentation was the highlight of a three-day annual state conference of the National Society, Daughters of the American Revolution (NSDAR). The Americanism Medal is awarded to an outstanding naturalized adult American citizen. In the 104-year history of the NSDAR, only seven other Americanism Medals have been awarded – Newman is the eight recipients.

Newman, her parents, two brothers, and sister escaped from Czechoslovakia when it was controlled by the communist government. She was only 11. The state had confiscated her father's bakery business because with 25 employees they considered it to be a capitalistic free enterprise – not permissible under the communist system.

The family was incarcerated in Budapest Hungry, for six months, (for escape), then they spent most of four years in displaced person camps in Germany, under deplorable condition.

Among the other things, she suffered frostbite, hunger, malnutrition, and near starvation. The family immigrated to the U.S.A. and all of them became naturalized American citizens.

Her marriage to Frank Charles Newman, a fellow Czech refugee and immigrant was prearranged by her parents when she was 19. Her husband rose from private to the rank of LTC in the U.S. Army. LTC Newman became a highly decorated master aviator and an Army Aviation unit commander. He was killed at Phu Bai, Vietnam during his second tour of duty there, shortly before he was scheduled to go home.

As a young widow, Newman was forced, by tragedy, to rear her three small children by herself in Ozark. Further tragedy befell when her son, Steven Allen "Chip" Newman, 17, was killed by a drunken driver while returning home from the beach in Florida. Another of her sons accidently drowned at Fort Rucker.

Newman is a supervisor of capital receptionists with the state of Alabama in Montgomery. On her own time, she is a patriotic, guest speaker on freedom, liberty, the opportunities of the American free enterprise system, and her personal testimony of how she was able to triumph over all the tragedies she and her family endured.

Newman somehow finds time to sponsor international officer students, primarily from the Czech Republic and Slovak Republic who come to Maxwell Air Force Base for special training at the U.S. Air Force's Air University.

"I just take them under my wing, like a mother hen, and treat them like my own son and like family. The Czech language is an exceedingly difficult one to learn, and it is nice for them to be able to communicate with someone in Czech when they are thousands of miles from home – for up to a year. My own family experienced the language barrier after we escaped, in Europe and in America as well. It's a strange feeling not to be able to tell people what you want or need, to exchange greetings and to express simple words of thanks and appreciation." Newman said.

IMAGES

Josef Honolke born September 21, 1869 in Austria. Lived till the age of 81. In 1950, buried in Neumarkt, Bavaria, Germany.

Bertha Hanke Honolke born August 5, 1889 in Austria. Lived till the age of 75. Died October 9, 1964, buried in Berchtesgaden, Bavaria, Germany.

Wilhelm (Willie) John Sr., Berta (Mother) and Helene Honolke

Rudolf Kralik born 1879 and Marie Anna Roubicek Kralik. Marie was born March 25, 1881 in Bohemia Europe. Parents of Jarmila Honolka.

1941 Jarmila Honolka on skies in Nova Paka, CZ

1945 Patricia, Eva and Don enjoy sledding in Nova Paka, CZ

1948 or 1949 Black Forest Schwarzwald, Germany - Don and Eva on ski team.

April 1995, Eva donates Lt. Colonel Frank C. Newman awards to permanent exhibit at the Aviation Museum in Prague, CR.

Eva Honolka Newman and Michael J. Novosel, Sr.
1971 United States Congressional Medal of Honor recipient

1940's Jarmila and John Honolka, Sr. in Prague Czechoslovakia

Picture was taken in 2011 when Don and Sharon Honolka went to the Czech Republic. This was the family home in the late 1940's in Trutnov, CZ. Patricia remembers the cellar being made into a partial garage by John., Sr. Don recalls his Grandparents, Berta and Josef living on the first floor. John Sr., and family lived on the second floor.

Picture was taken in 2011 in Pilnikov, Czechoslovakia. John Sr.'s business from 1945 "Koruna Fancy Pastries". We were told a portion of the building has been converted into apartments.

Picture taken 2011 Cousins Barbara Rauscher, Don Honolka and Hans Honolke.

August 2007 - Hans Honolke visits cousins in Arlington, TX. L-R, Tom, John Jr., Don, Eva, Patricia Honolka and Hans Honolke.

Eva loved having fun

*1948 or 49 leaving prison
in Budapest, Hungry.
Don, Eva Patricia and John, Jr. Honolka*

*1950 Family Passport picture.
Eva, Don, John Sr., John Jr.,
Patricia, Jarmila and infant Tom*

Saying good-bye to Oma, Bertha Honolke, at railroad station, just prior to family boarding ship to America. How they must have felt, not knowing if they would ever see Oma again. Don, Eva, John Sr., Oma, Jarmila, Patricia, John Jr., and Tom.

Reunited in 1970 Mother, Berta and son, John Honolka, Sr. in Berchtesgaden, Germany

Family boards USS General Harry Taylor. Lower left corner. Sailed from Bremerhaven, German through the English Channel to South America. Porta de Cabedello, Brazil. Continuing to New Orleans, LA.

1989 Eva Honolka Newman displays her numerous passports

Farm home in Protivin, IA. Picture taken by Suzanne Honolka
Dudek, July 2005. Family could not live there in the winter
because home had no electricity or running water.

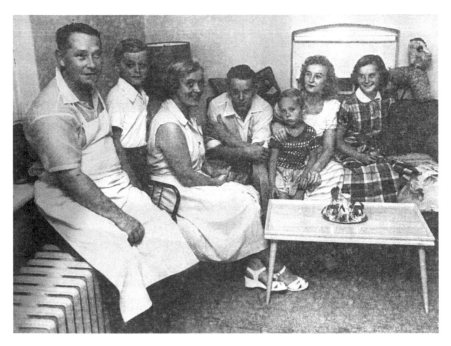

September 25, 1955 from the article posted in The Cedar Rapids Gazette. John Sr., in his bakery apron, John Jr., Jarmila, Don, Eva, toddler Tom and Patricia.

Mid 1950 Amana Bakery in Amana, Iowa

Mid 1950's John Honolka, Sr. built Amana Society Bakery to 18 routes plus individual distributers from Atlanta, Georgia to Dallas, TX. John., Sr. and Don in photo.

July 7, 1956 Mr. and Mrs. Frank Charles Newman

1965, Frank, Steven "Chip", Julie, Mike, and Eva Newman.

LTC Frank C. Newman
Westville Memorial Cemetery
in Ozark, Alabama

Westview Cemetery Ozark, Alabama

*1970 Major General Delk M. Oden, Maxwell Air Force Base.
Presenting earned medals of LTC Frank Charles Newman.
Steven "Chip", Mike, Julie and Eva Honolka.*

*1987 August 26th Don, Eva, Patricia, Tom and John Jr. Honolka.
This picture was taken after Jarmila Honolka's memorial service.*

August 1999 Family Reunion in Kansas, Eva, Don, Patricia, John, Jr. and Tom

October 2001 Family Reunion in Montgomery, AL.
L-R Don, John Jr., Eva, Patricia, and Tom

October 2004 Family Reunion in Arlington, TX L-R
John Jr., Eva, Don, Tom and Patricia

Eva Honolka Newman was awarded with the Cross of Merit of the Czech Minister of Defense, 3ʳᵈ Class, for her significant merit in the development of the Ministry of Defense of the Czech Republic on August 19, 2015 at a ceremony held at the Maxwell Air Force base in Montgomery, Alabama.

Cross of Merit

*Brigadier General Jiri Verner,
Defense Military and Air Attaché
of the Czech Republic decorates
Mrs. Eva Honolka Newman.*

"Eva overcame her life suffering through offering unconditional love and belief to all."
Air Force Major General Bohuslav Dvorak and Miroslava Dvorakova, Prague CR

Eva Honolka Newman honored for sponsoring Officers in
training. Maxwell Airforce Base, Montogomery, Alabama

1996 March 30ᵗʰ Ft. Rucker Women's History Month

Eva served as a receptionist and tour guide at the State Capital and the First White House of the Confederacy for 33 years.

Eva Honolka Newman in front of the State Capitol of Alabama

State Capitol – Montgomery, Alabama

Jarmila and John Honolka,
Sr.,Westview Cemetery
in Ozark, Alabama

May 14, 1937 – September 13, 2020

Westview Cemetery Ozark, Alabama

1994 Former Cedar Rapids Woman Wins Citizen Medal

The Cedar Rapids Gazette, Friday, March 25, 1994
By: Lynn M. Tefft, Gazette Staff Writer

A former Cedar Rapids woman and Czech native has been awarded the Daughters of the American Revolution Americanism Medal, which recognizes outstanding adult naturalized American Citizens.

Eva Honolka Newman, 53, came to the United States from Czechoslovakia with her family in 1951.

The family's bakery in Czechoslovakia had been confiscated by authorities after being labeled capitalistic, and the family also had been incarcerated in Hungry after unsuccessfully trying to escape once before.

The family spent a few months in Cresco but was uncomfortable and on the verge of returning home when Czechs from Cedar Rapids area contacted them.

Newman and her family then moved to Cedar Rapids, where she attended St. Wenceslaus High School and worked at a bakery in Czech Village.

She moved to Amana and helped her parents open a bakery in 1956, but still attended St. Wenceslaus.

She was named queen of the Czech Festival and participated in the Miss Iowa pageant.

A painting Newman created while she was a student at Coe College has been displayed at Christmas time for many years at St. Wenceslaus.

After she became a naturalized citizen, Newman married a fellow Czech immigrant at age 19.

Because her husband was a military officer, she moved around the country for many years, settling down in Ozark, AL., after her husband was killed in Vietnam.

Two of her three sons also died young in separate accidents.

Currently a supervisor of receptionists at the state Capitol in Montgomery, AL. Newman spends her free time speaking to civic groups about freedom, liberty, and free enterprise.

She uses personal testimony to show how these principles help people triumph over tragedy.

Newman also sponsors international officer students who come from the Czech and Slovak republics to Maxwell Air Force Base in Montgomery, as well as hosting other visitors from her native country.

1994 Czech Refugee Family Members
Return Home After 44 Years

Prague, Czech Republic – September 1994
By: A. Dwain Williams, Photographer/Photojournalist/Author

When John and Jarmila Honolka escaped from Czechoslovakia in 1948 with their four children they expected to return in about two years, after the communist form of government had burned itself out. Neither of them lived to see freedom and democracy in their beloved homeland, some 42 years later. Two of their five children did. Patricia of Kansas, and her older sister Eva Honolka Newman, of Montgomery, Alabama returned to what is now the Czech Republic for a two week walk down memory lane in August 1994.

"Amazingly, nothing has really changed that much in all these years" said Eva Newman. "The house where I was born, in Trutnov in 1937 is still there, and people are still living in it. My father's factory and bakery look just like it did when we escaped. It was confiscated by the government without any compensation and was never returned to my family. It's now being used as a beauty shop, school kitchen, and for apartments".

The Honolka family was caught and imprisoned, for escape, for six months in Budapest, Hungary in a place called Tolinshaus. John Honolka was separated from his family, beaten, and grossly abused at the hands of his captors. Conditions there were deplorable, with over 500 women and children crowded in together in one large room. There was truly little food and water, filthy toilet facilities. And only a weekly shower. The prison was infested with roaches and other vermin. The captors placed little value on human lives, especially the little babies and children of the political prisoners.

The next line typed by A. Dwain Williams was TO BE CONTINUED. No continuation was located.

1995 A Soldier's Story

Montgomery Advertiser – May 29, 1995
By: Frank Mastin Jr. – Advertiser Staff Writer

Eva Newman visits the grave of her husband at a cemetery in Ozark in 1990. LTC Frank Charles Newman was killed in a helicopter crash just five days before his second tour of duty in Vietnam was to end.

If LTC Frank Charles Newman is looking down from heaven this Memorial Day, he must be pleased to see that his widow, Eva, has dedicated her life to keeping his memory and spirit alive.

He was killed in Vietnam in 1970, with less than a week remaining in his second tour.

Col. Newman escaped communism in his native Czechoslovakia in 1949 by fleeing to Germany, where he was put into a displaced person's camp.

Such camps were common in Europe in the years after World War II as people driven from their homes by communism tried to make their way to a new life.

Probably few people hated communism more than Frank Charles Newman.

He entered Karl University in Prague at age 16, bent on becoming a Catholic priest. He became fluent in Latin, English, German, French, Russian and Polish. He went on to study law and the great philosophers, such as Plato, Socrates, and Karl Marx.

While in the German camp, he tried unsuccessfully to organize an underground effort to overthrow the communists. When that failed, he enlisted in the U.S. Army while still in the camp.

His enlistment became his ticket to the United States. He arrived on U.S. soil in 1952 and was assigned to Fort Sill, Oklahoma.

The year before Mr. Newman's escape from Czechoslovakia, another Czech family, John and Jarmila Honolka and their four children, had begun their own journey to freedom. One of the Honolkas' children was 13-year-old Eva.

Life had not been easy for the Honolkas. In 1948, they fled Czechoslovakia through Hungary to reach Austria, but they were caught at the Austrian border by Czech police and thrown into prison in Budapest.

When they arrived in Budapest, Mr. Honolka was separated from his family and sent to a re-education camp elsewhere in Hungary to be indoctrinated in communism.

Eight months later, Mrs. Honolka escaped from the prison with the children and fled to Austria, where they were placed in a displaced person's camp. It became their home for two years.

"People in displaced person camps are lost causes," Mrs. Newman said. "They don't belong to their homeland. They do not belong to the country where the camp is, and they do not know where they are going. They don't know who is going to take them in."

Mr. Honolka, with no knowledge of his family's whereabouts, escaped from the re-education camp in Hungry after 11 months and traveled to Austria, where he began a search.

Aided by an Austrian lawyer and the International Red Cross, Mr. Honolka found his family at a displaced person's camp in Salzburg, Austria. After World War II, Austria remained neutral during the Cold War. Refugees who flooded across that country's borders were often detained.

Mr. Honolka and his family planned a daring escape from the Austrian camp in 1950 and entered Germany.

Although Eva was only an adolescent and unaware of it at the time, the man she eventually would marry was a ward of the same German camp.

By 1951, the Honolkas had found a sponsor in Iowa, and set out for a new life in America.

A year later, Mr. Newman, then an enlisted man in the United States Army, was transferred to Fort Sill, Oklahoma.

He was commissioned as a second lieutenant in the artillery. He went on to become a command pilot capable of flying all the helicopters and fixed-winged aircraft used by the Army. He attained the rank of lieutenant colonel.

LTC Newman was killed in the crash of his Army Mohawk reconnaissance aircraft at Phu Bai, Vietnam on Feb. 24, 1970 – five days before he was scheduled to complete his second tour in Vietnam. He was 42.

He is buried in an Ozark, Alabama cemetery, in the town where he had bought a home and planned to settle down with Mrs. Newman and their three children.

Starting Over

The end of his life marked a new beginning of a new era. Mrs. Newman, who dedicated herself to perpetuating the ideals her husband held dear – duty, honor, country, God, and family.

Now a supervisor of the State Capital Receptionist, Mrs. Newman recently recalled how she and Colonel Newman came to be married in 1956.

"I had a pre-arranged marriage by my parents," she said. She had just received a scholarship to an art institute in Chicago after graduation from high school.

"I was 18 years old and my father did not feel that a young woman, 18 years of age should be in a big city like Chicago by herself," Mrs. Newman said.

"He felt like it would be better for me to marry an honorable man, and he knew just the very one – and he was Frank Charles Newman.

Mrs. Newman said her father told her that she had met her soon-to-be-husband at the camp in Germany about six years earlier. Her parents had become friends with Mr. Newman in the camp. Eva was 11 years old, then and Mr. Newman was 22.

Cold Feet

Mrs. Newman was not happy about the pre-arranged marriage, but she was raised to honor her mother and father.

"I was young and foolish and believed that a girl (first) fell madly in love and sailed into the sunset with Prince Charming." Mrs. Newman said.

"On the fourth of July 1956, my father put me on an airplane and sent me to Austin, Texas, to marry Frank Charles Newman," she said.

Instead of heading to college, Eva Honolka was a frightened young woman, alone on a plane, headed west to marry a man she did not know. She did what any young woman would do in a similar situation: She cried.

She had gotten some last-minute advice from her mother before boarding the plane.

"I said, 'I don't want to get married, mamma.' My mother said, 'Eva, if you marry out of love, you have thin glasses on your eyes. You do not see reality. And sometime when you take them off and you do see reality, it's not all gold that glitters.'"

The marriage took place in a Catholic Church in Texas, on July 7, 1956, Mrs. Newman said.

"We went back to our apartment, and I want to tell you that rigor mortis set in," Mrs. Newman said.

An intelligent and perceptive man, Mr. Newman made allowances for his new bride's feelings, beginning on their wedding night.

He suggested that she sleep in the bedroom, he would sleep on sofa, and that they begin a period of courtship.

'A Gentleman"

"He was smart enough to know that he had to give me some time to get to know him, and it worked out just fine," she said.

"And for the next three months, even though we were married, he just dated me." Mrs. Newman said.

Three months after the wedding, the marriage was consummated after Mr. Newman received orders to ship out to Korea for 18 months, she said.

When Col. Newman went off to Korea, Mrs. Newman went to live with her parents in Iowa.

"He wrote to me every single day he was away from me." For the entire 18 months, Mrs. Newman said.

"And I want you to know that when we were together, if he went on a trip overnight, he wrote.

"On the day he was killed he had written me a letter." She said.

"Every single day that man was away from me, he wrote to me, and that is what keeps on making me tell this story," Mrs. Newman said, 'because I think it was above and beyond the call of duty."

Treasured Letters

Mrs. Newman said she still has all the letters and has numbered them in the order of the dates they were written.

Among the letters is one written during his first tour in Vietnam, when Col. Newman was hiding under his helicopter after it has crashed, and he was surrounded by the Viet Cong.

"He didn't think he was going to make it out of there alive," she said. "The monsoon season was in full force, and he crawled under the helicopter. He found a scrap of paper and wrote on it, 'I am writing you today to let you know that under all conditions and circumstances I love you and our children.'"

But good fortune was with the colonel that time, and he was rescued. One of the first things he did when he reached safety was to write a regular letter in which he enclosed the message he had written underneath the helicopter, Mrs. Newman said.

"Basically, Frank Newman made me who I am today," Mrs. Newman said.

The Newman's had four children. The first child died during childbirth, and one son, Steven Alan, was killed by a drunken driver. Mrs. Newman said. The surviving children are Michael David of Atlanta, and Julie Ann Slaten of Birmingham.

Mrs. Newman spends a lot of time on the speaking circuit delivering her message about patriotism, God, and family. She is propelled, she said, by a series of occurrences in her life.

Her son, 17-year-old Steven was killed June 14, 1980, on Flag Day, which also was Michael's 21st birthday. Her only grandchild was born on Memorial Day 1991

Mrs. Newman's second grandchild is due next month, on Flag Day.

"I know the Lord has a mission for my life." Mrs. Newman said, "and my mission just happens to be red, white and blue – God, duty, honor and country.

"I feel like wherever my husband quit his mission, it was given to me to pick it up and carry it on."

1995 EHN Helps CR Commemorate End of WWII In Europe

April 1995, Prague-Kbely, Czech Republic

At the invitation of the Czech Government, Eva Honolka Newman, from Montgomery, Alabama, former resident of Ozark, Alabama, was a guest of honor here at dedication ceremonies at the Air Museum at 10:00 a.m. April 27th.

A new Exposition was opened, to commemorate the end of World War II in Europe. Mrs. Newman was born in Trutnov, Czechoslovakia, and her family escaped in 1948 and eventually immigrated to the U.S.A. She is a recipient of the prestigious "Americanism" Medal, awarded her in 1994, by the Daughters of the American Revolution (NSDAR).

Also dedicated was a permanent exhibit of medals, memorabilia, and the uniforms of LTC Frank C. Newman. His medals and decorations include the Legion of Merit, Distinguished Flying Cross, The Bronze Star, Purple Heart, Air Medal with 19 Oak Leaf Clusters and numerous others, including uniforms.

Mrs. Newman's husband who was killed in Vietnam. The items were all donated by Mrs. Newman and her two children. Col. Newman was born in Nepomuk, Czechoslovakia and was also a refugee. He joined the U.S. Army as a private and served 17 years before his death in a plane crash in February 1970, while he was Commanding Officer of the 101st Aviation Company. He was a Master Aviator, and a highly decorated "Mustang" officer.

Other highlights of the ceremonies were the meeting of graduates of military schools and courses at Lackland Air Force Base, Texas and Maxwell Air Force Base, Alabama, USA, with the Minister of Defense of the Czech Republic, Dr. Vilem Holan and other distinguished guests.

Major General Frantisek Vana, First Deputy Minister of Defense
Mr. Lubos Dobrovsky, Protocol office of President Havel

The United States Embassy Representatives
Military to Military Team Representatives
Colonel Vladimir Remek, Czech Cosmonaut and Director of the Air
    Museum
Major General Zezula, Chief of the Personnel Department
Mgr. Klucina, Chief of the Historical Institute
Colonel Jiri Prchal, Graduate of the Air War College, Maxwell Air
    Force Base
Colonel Jiri Moravee, Mg. Editor, Aviatik magazine and Guest Speaker
Teachers of the Brno Military Academy
LTC Rudi Peleska, Graduate of Air Command and Staff College
Other Czech Officers who have graduated from United States military
    courses.

Mrs. Newman was treated to a piano concert of classical music of
Check composer Dvorak at the Chapel of Mirrors here, as the guest of
Czech Cosmonaut, Colonel Vladimir, and Mrs. Jana Remik, Colonel
Jiri Moravec treated Mrs. Newman to an aerial view of Czech historic
sites of her native country from a small private airplane. Highlighting
her one-week trip was a tour of the City of Brno and the Cathedral
of Saint Peter and Paul, as a guest of Colonel George and Eva Prchal.

The text of Eva Honolka Newman's speech follows:

Honorable Minister of Defense, Dr. Vilem Holan, Ladies, Gentlemen,
and Special Guest:

On this day of the meeting of the Minister of Defense, Dr. Vilem
Holan with Czech graduates of military schools and courses in the
United States, I am honored to participate with you in this stirring and
remarkable occasion; the opening of the new exposition celebrating
the 50th anniversary of the end of World War II at the aviation museum
here in Prague-Kbelich.

In my lifetime, I did not think the time would come when I would
see freedom banners spread across Eastern Europe like butterflies

struggling in flight. Voices joined, growing more confident with each step; energized by the magical word, freedom.

In 1951 our family went to the U.S.A. as refugees from Czechoslovakia. We arrived there hungry, torn, scarred, and scared, but there was the promise of opportunity to follow happiness with hope:

To have the dignity of work

To praise our God

To have freedom to Love our fellow human beings.

To be of SERVICE

To appreciate life as it was given to us by a power beyond ourselves.

We are grateful to the nation that so graciously adopted us – the United States of America.

I work as the supervisor of Capitol receptionists and guides in Montgomery, Alabama. I have greeted and seen thousands of people from many countries, but not from the Czech Republic. It was not until 1992, when Maxwell Air Force Base received officers from the Czech Republic in study at the International Officers School, Squadron Officer School, Air Command and Staff College, and the Air War College.

These are bright, intelligent men; eager to learn and to take home valuable lessons of leadership, trustworthiness, patriotism, and history, to help them steer the fledgling new republic towards liberty and freedom with new ideas.

I pray that these bright minds will continue their quest for liberty; to pass on what they have learned, so freedom can continue to flourish. We know that it will not be a good world for any of us until it becomes a good world for all of us.

Each one teaches one, and each ten teach ten, that liberated people determine their own future.

Freedom is not just a choice or an opportunity, it is an obligation to respect the truth of our moral identity. We must meet that obligation and the sacrifices for freedom before we can claim its' privileges and benefits.

I wish to convey to the Czech people how proud they should be of their military officers, for how diligently they are working, with much enthusiasm and energy, with willingness to learn new principles and concepts of liberty. They should be given every opportunity to teach others and to share the lessons learned, so that the Czech Nation can reach new heights of a good life that it so rightly deserves.

During this valuable opening ceremony of the new Exposition of the Aviation Museum, I am dedicating to the Czech people, medals, memorabilia, and uniforms of a U.S. Army Aviator, a "Mustang" Officer who worked himself through the ranks of the military – LTC Frank Charles Newman.

Frank was born in Nepomuk, Czechoslovakia. He lived amidst fear of the second World War and later in fear of the oppression of Communism.

He came to the U.S. with a lot of hope and a lot of aspiration in his heart, but with truly little else. Through long days and hard work, he gained American Citizenship.

He enlisted in the U.S. Army, in Germany. He worked himself through the ranks, from a Private (E1) to become a Commissioned Officer of the 101st Aviation Company when he was killed.

I say that with a great deal of pride for our nation – the U.S.A., because the promise of opportunity was fulfilled again when a man was given the chance to follow happiness with hope.

Frank was my better half, my partner in life, the father of our children. Five days before he was scheduled to go home from his second tour of duty in Vietnam, he lost his life there.

I became a widow, with three little children, two boys and a girl, and when the time came, I pinned Frank's wings on my son's chest, and I was proud to be the wife of a soldier who gave his all.

Frank's ultimate dream was to see the Czech people free; to have democracy as once experienced for 20-years under President Tomas Garique Masarik. Frank was a son of two nations; he never forgot his homeland, and he was also faithful to the nation that adopted him.

Because of his love for the Czech people, I feel it appropriate and I feel incredibly grateful that his humble possessions will be a part of the museum. We can start building bridges of respect and admiration – one nation to another, join hands as brothers and sisters and walk on this place called "Earth". Memories are not just imprinting of the past upon us – they are the keeper of what is meaningful for our deepest hopes and dreams.

1996 Department of Army

National Women's History Month
February 20, 1996

History looks different when the contributions of women are included. Keynote speaker: Eva Honolka Newman.

Mrs. Eva H. Newman is Supervisor of Capitol Receptionists, with the State of Alabama in Montgomery.

Mrs. Newman was born Eva Honolka in Trutnov, Czechoslovakia. Her family immigrated to Iowa after World War II.

She married Frank C. Newman, also of Czech heritage, and they had three sons and a daughter. Her husband served as a Foreign Military Liaison Officer at Fort Rucker, AL. He was killed in a 1970 plane crash during his second tour in Vietnam, and is buried in Ozark, AL.

Mrs. Newman began her public speaking career while still in high school and has made hundreds of appearances since then. Mrs. Newman's awards include the prestigious "Americanism Medal" by the Daughters of the American Revolution (NSDAR) at Birmingham, Al in 1994. That same year she was awarded the "Sustained Superior" honor for volunteerism in Montgomery, AL.

Under the Alabama Goodwill Ambassador Program, Mrs. Newman sponsors visiting Czech Air Force Officers and their families who are assigned to Maxwell Air Force Base, AL for training. In April of 1995, she was invited by the government of the Czech Republic to be guest speaker and guest of honor at special commemoration ceremonies at the Aviation Museum in Prague. This was the celebration of the 50th Anniversary of the end of World War II in Europe (VE Day). A special permanent exhibit was dedicated, honoring her late husband.

Mrs. Newman makes her home in Montgomery, AL.

1999 Freedom Is Not Free

The Times – Recorder Fayette County's Newspaper
Volume XXIII Number 9 – Wednesday, October 13, 1999
By: Anita Parker, R-R Associate Editor

Eva Honolka Newman likely appreciates the truth of the statement better than most people. Born in Trutnov, Czechoslovakia, in 1937, she survived the bombing of her home country, oppression by the Nazis during World War II and the Communists later, and incarceration when her family was captured during their escape.

Freedom is not something she will ever take for granted; Mrs. Newman told the audience who had gathered to hear her speak at the Fayette Area Career/Technical School. Newman's appearance was part of the "Patriotism, God, and Country" program sponsored Monday night by the Fayette County Enrichment Parents' Association.

Newman said she is "concerned today about the Land of the Free, because many people don't understand that freedom can be taken away in the course of one election."

The importance of freedom and liberty cannot be overstated, she said, especially to someone who spent so much of her childhood without either.

"I have looked into the face of hell," she said. "It's not a nice word, but it describes what I have seen happen, what humanity does when an important factor is left out of their lives, religion and faith."

Many in the audience Monday night were children, and Newman clearly affected them with descriptions of the bombing and oppression she remembers from her childhood.

My main emotion when I was your age was fear," she told them. "I was afraid to go to school, because if the bombs fell while we were there, we might all be buried alive. When the students were all crammed in the basement together and the bombs would fall, you could hear the panes falling out of the windows. And I was afraid to go home because what if the bombs had destroyed your neighborhood and killed your family? Then someone would come from the government and take you to an orphanage."

She said lines for bread and milk were so long that you would have to stand there for hours, and then the supplies might run out before you got to the window.

The Nazis would also periodically search the homes of the Czechoslovakian citizens, looking for Bibles, radios, and extra food over the allocation you got from the government.

You weren't supposed to have a Bible because everyone knew God didn't exist, right?" she said. "and you weren't supposed to have a radio, because you might hear news from England or America about how the war was going."

Her father kept a radio and a Bible hidden in the rafters of their home. Newman said, and he and a group of men would gather every two weeks to read scriptures and listen to the news of the war.

Although she was always terrified the Nazis would find the Bible or the radio, it was extra food in the pantry that led to tragedy during one such inspection.

"Every person got a certain amount of food stamps, and if you ran out before the month was over, you just didn't get any more food," she said. "But there were farmers that produced food, and if you were brave enough to go out at night, you could buy food from them. This was called the black market."

Her father had just bought a sausage from a farmer on the black market, Newman Said, and when the Nazis came to search the house, they found it. They knew it was not on the family's food stamp allocation, and they held a gun to her father's head and forced him to tell them where he bought it.

Then they handcuffed her father, took him to the farmer's house, forced the farmer's whole family to come outside, "and they hung him in front of his family and my father." Newman said.

She told of many other horrors her family and their neighbors were forced to endure during the war, and their brief optimism at war's end.

"But the war ended in 1945, and in 1948, we had a brand-new oppressive government called Communism," she said, adding that the government was able to come to power in part because not many people exercised their right to vote in the elections that followed the war.

In Communism, she said, "no individual is responsible for himself. Everything belongs to a cooperative society."

When the government seized her father's pastry business, he was jailed for three months because he refused to let the Communists send him away for "re-education." After he was released from jail, he decided to escape with his wife and four children. They got to Budapest, Hungary, before being captured.

"We were taken to a prison in Budapest, where my mother and we children were all put in a cell with 500 other women and children," she said. "My father was taken away from us and "sent to be re-educated."

Newman said she, her mother, and siblings stayed in the prison for a year, sleeping on beds of straw infested with fleas, ticks, and roaches. Then they escaped and boarded a train to Vienna, Austria. They were almost caught by guards who were checking for passports before they reached their destination.

"My mother got down on her knees, folded her hands in prayer, and begged, "In the name of God and for the sake of these children, please let us pass." Newman recalled.

The guards were moved by her plea and allowed the family to continue their journey. When they arrived in Vienna, they were hosted in a displaced person's camp.

"It was a lot like the images of the camps in Kosovo that you've seen on television." She said.

There was little food available and they were forced "to catch rats and mice to eat in order to survive," she said.

"You might think. I would never do that," she said. "But let me tell you, when it comes to survival, you will."

Her father, who had been working in labor camps, was eventually reunited with the rest of the family by the Red Cross.

When he arrived at the displaced persons camp, his cheeks were sunken in and he was so thin she hardly recognized him, Newman said.

"He had been hung by his wrists and beaten so severely that his back was permanently scarred," she said.

But after three and a half years the family, now with the addition of a little brother born in the camp, was scheduled to emigrate to New Zealand.

"At the last moment, they told us we would be going to the United States," she said.

They boarded a ship for New Orleans and arrived after a three-week trip in rough seas.

Mrs. Newman was married at age 19 to Frank C. Newman, a fellow Czech refugee. Her family had met Newman in Germany at a displaced person's camp.

He joined the U.S. Army, rising to the rank of LTC, but was killed in a 1970 plane crash in Vietnam. One of her sons, Steven, was killed by a drunk driver at the age of 17.

Mrs. Newman had six children, five sons and a daughter. One son and a daughter survive.

I've had an eventful life," Newman said. "some call it a tragic life. I have buried four sons, and my husband died in Vietnam. I had cancer and lost my voice. I was never supposed to be able to speak again. But by the grace of God, here I am. By the grace of God, all things are possible."

Newman said she has dedicated herself to "paying back" the nation that adopted her and her family when they were refugees.

Her efforts have earned her the Americanism Medal, presented by the Daughters of the American Revolution in Birmingham, and the Sustained Superior Honor for volunteerism in Montgomery, where she makes her home and works for the state government as Supervisor of Capitol Receptionists.

Newman would tell you that mostly her job is to make others aware of the importance of voting, of participating in the selection of your government and the passage of its laws, and, above all "how wonderful it is to be free."

2000 Veterans of Foreign Wars

Montgomery, Alabama

I want to thank you for giving me the honor to be here with you tonight. I hope I will contribute to your gathering, so you will be able to say "You just didn't spend some time here but invested in it.

I came to this country as a refugee from Czechoslovakia. As a child my life experience was the 2nd World War (WWII). Then, in 1948 our family escaped from the oppression of comminism. We were caught on the border of Austria and imprisoned for one year in Budapest, Hungary. Our Mother and her four children escaped again from prison and lived two years in displaced person camps.

On a daily basis, I am grateful that Providence meant for us to be here in the United States of America and that this country (America) so graciously adopted us.

In the eighteenth century America could be described as a loose group of weak and scattered colonies. We were at the time a free and compassionate society, committed to the preservation of Liberty and human values.

The impact of religion on American life is to stand erect and with dignity as a Child of God. I submit to you that our deep faith is every man's right, and as a Christian, drawing upon the riches within our faith and by remembering who we are, and what we are as Americans.

We need to rouse our national consciences in this nation, as to whether or not we are going to finish up in any ways worthy of its' beginning. I say educate, educate, educate.

I am a new American and in my hands I hold a priceless heritage; mine is the splendor of the past and the shining future of a citizen of these the United States, my home.

We the people, both Men and Women must decide through experience, perhaps even disillusionment what is a genuinely good life.

Personally, I feel the individual responsibility to teach and share patriotism, for the sake of liberty and the good life as well. I am proud to be an American. I have paid the dues to be a Citizen of these the United States. To see anyone burning the flag truly upsets me. When the unwilling, led by the unknowing, are doing the impossible for the ungrateful who descrate the flag it deeply offends me.

You see, somewhere in the World beats the heart of an American Army Soldier, Marine, Airman, Sailor; and here at home a Mother, a wife, a Sweetheart and Family anxiouly wait for their return home.

I understand those feelings. Thirty years ago I also waited. I am a Gold Star Wife. On panel 13, line 52 is the name of LTC Frank C. Newman, my husband and the father of Michael, Julie and Steven Newman.

Frank was born in Czechoslovakia, where he grew up admist strife and hunger. He lived amidst fear of the 2nd World War and late of communism. He came to the United States with a lot of hope and a lot of aspirations in his heart, but very little else. He could not speak the English language, but through long days of hard work he learned the language and gained his American citizenship that he had yearned for.

Frank Charles Newman enlisted in the United State Sarmy, as a Private and worked himself up the ranks from E-1 to be a LTC (O-5). That's what's called a "Mustang Officer". He did that in 17 years and also became a Master Aviator. During his second tour in Vietnam in 1970 he was the Commander of the 131st Aviation Company, First Aviation Brigade at Phu Bai.

I say this with a great deal of pride for our nation, because only in a Country as the United States is such anything possible for a refugee to become a Commander in its' military. It was a promise if opportunity, fulfilled. I pinned those wings on my son's chest, and I was proud to be an American.

What hurt me most was the silence of the majority, who turned away without verifying the scarifices we had made in conflict that wasn't even declared a war.

When this nation handed me the folded American flag, as a token from a grateful nation, I made a promise; "You were willing to defend and die fot this Country, I am willing to live and serve this Country."

We cannot buy freedom with poster paints and flag burning; we buy freedom with great scarifice, I have seen "Old Glory" flying at half mast, in Arlington National Cemetery. I heard a bugle played as a veteran was laid to rest, but it was not until I stood at the Vietnam Memorial Wall and laid three red roses there, on for each of my children, in honor of their Dad, that I realized the intense feelings of what it really means to be an American.

Yes, I am a citizen of the greatest nation on Earth. I am proud to be an American.

A nation was born and became great because of the ideals and principals in which our Founding Fathers so deeply believed and out soldiers fought for so tenacacioyusly.

It is Bunker Hill, Lexington, Saratogo, Yorktown, Italy, Normandy, The battle fo the Bulge, France, Germany, Guadalcanal, the south Pacific, Iwo Jima and all of World War II, Korea, Vietnam and the Gulf War; just to name a few.

As a nation, we paid the supreme sacrifice and each one of us has to teach one and each ten teach ten. We must teach our younger generation the glorious hertiage of our brave men and women, When you go home, tell them of us, for their tomorrows we gave up our today.

When our family came here as refugees we walked down the gangplank from the ship. The attitude of those who greeted us was "You want to be an American? You will first have to learn and understand America. Is that asking too much today? When I was studying the Declaration of Independence and the Constitution I was in awe of the noble ideas those Americans believed in. It caused me to redouble my efforts in the study of English, so that I could better understand my new hertiage.

We defend our hertiage when we seek the faith of our fathers. We become living examples of our total hertiage, from one generation to the next. The faith of our fathers lives and has lived through the brutality of war.

It is that quality of men and women which, in a hour of strain, do the just, and if possible, the generous thing.

I want to thank each and every one of you Patriots, from the bottom of my heart; for serving our Country. I will never forget the price you have paid so we can all enjoy liberty. Every day should like the glorious 4th of July in 1776. We are people of many faiths and many races; that is the genius of America. Epluribus Unum (Out of many, one)

Remember, Service is the rent we pay for our room on Earth.

God Bless you all.

2001 Czech Refugee Finds Paths
to Freedom & Liberty
Painful and Difficult, But Rewarding

The Montgomery Independent July 26, 2011
By: A. Dwain Williams

For Eva Honolka Newman and the rest of the John and Jarmila Honolka family, the dream to celebrate Independence Day and to experience freedom and opportunity began over 4\53 years ago in Trutnov, Czechoslovakia. Mrs. Newman was only 11 years old at that time. and remembers vividly the horrors and fears of World War II as well as the Nazi occupation of her native country. "On VE day we rejoiced to be rid of the Nazis and were filled with hope of freedom and democracy. Before too many months passed, we had free elections, unfortunately a small percentage of the people took the effort to vote. Before we knew it, we were under a totalitarian co-op form of government that replaced our flag with a communist flag; a yellow hammer and cycle on a red background, she said".

"No one can genuinely appreciate how precious and wonderful freedom, liberty, and individual opportunities are unless they have lived without them. After the war, my father built a successful bakery business, and employed about 30 people. The new government classified my Dad as a capitalist, and confiscated his business, without any compensation. When my father strenuously objected and refused to become a communist, he was arrested and put into jail, for conspiracy against the state. He was strung up by his wrists and beaten with heavy leather straps. Our family nightmares and dreams of a better life started all over again at that time. When the government let my Dad out of jail, through the help of the underground, he arranged for the family to escape.

"Tragically, we were caught on the border of Hungary and put into prison in Budapest before escaping. For almost a year we suffered from hunger, humiliation, despair, and deprivation. Human life meant truly little to our captors; there were about 500 women and children in one large open room with scant toilet facilities. The little babies that died from malnutrition and disease were carried out and buried, unceremoniously, in paper bags by the prison guards."

"We then lived-in displaced person camps in Germany for three years, as refugees. Conditions there were pretty bad; my two brothers, sister and I all suffered from malnutrition as a reminder of just how bad it was in the camps."

My father was obsessed with the hope of emigrating to America, the land of freedom and opportunity. We talked about it, we dreamed about it, we fantasized about it, and we prayed for it to happen. We had walked away from our home, our friends, and our roots, with only the clothes on our back, in search of freedom.

"Finally, in 1951 we had a sponsor and approval to the United States of America. We went by ship and landed at New Orleans, then went by train to Cresco, Iowa. We were met by our American sponsor, a corn farmer, and his wife. We rode to our new "Home" on the back of a flatbed truck out into the 'Boondocks". 'Home' was an old weather-beaten farmhouse that the cows had lived in during the winter months. There was no running water, toilet facilities, gas, or electricity in the house, but there was an outhouse and a water well outside. The basement was full of water, and we had to shovel the "Cow Chips" out of the house before we could even live there. All we could see for miles in every direction was 500 acres of barren fields, to be plowed, planted, and cultivated", and my family was brought there to do that in return for our passage from Germany."

"There is no way I can relate to you exactly how it felt when we arrived at our destination, even though it was America and freedom. We had all imagined, hoped, and dreamed of luxurious surroundings, a nice home, a nice car, and golden opportunity. We had nothing, we came there destitute, obligated, broken, torn, anxious, and hungry. We had no means of transportation and the nearest farm was miles and miles away. We were almost like indentured servants. We asked ourselves

"What now"? We could not go back to the camps; we were stuck. The situation was so bad that it broke my Mother's heart, partly because she came from a classy family. It was such as disappointment to her that she never really ever got over it."

"My Dad, John Honolka, was an honorable man, trustworthy, tenacious, a hard task master, disciplined, and a dedicated parent. He was my role model. He once shared his philosophy of work with me, he said 'An aggressive man will work today and play tomorrow, but a lazy man will play today and work tomorrow. A twelve-hour day is only half a day's work.

"We stuck it out on the farm that summer of 1951, but we knew we could not survive a northern Iowa winter under those austere conditions. With the help of the Chamber of Commerce in Cedar Rapids, and the Milo Naxera family, we moved to Cedar Rapids, worked there, and went to school. Dad worked two and three jobs to support his family of five children, we all worked, and we worked hard, long hours".

John Honolka's big opportunity finally came in 1955 when he was hired to manage the Amana bakery at the Amana Colonies in Amana, Iowa. He built the business into a thriving productive, and profitable million-dollar operation. He increased sales almost 1,000 percent by 1966. At the peak of production, the bakery distributed bread in eight states in the Midwest, via refrigerated trucks. "He found the streets of America were paved with gold, but the gold was freedom, liberty, and opportunity. All of us became Naturalized American citizens. None of us became rich and famous but we all have lived to realize the American dream, have become successful, and enjoyed over 53 years of freedom and individual opportunity" she said.

"A stroll down memory lane is not always a pleasant walk; sometimes it brings back painful and deep emotions. Going back to Cedar Rapids, attending my 40th high school reunion at Amana, and going back to the old farmhouse near Protivin recently was a bittersweet trip for me.

I buried my first son at Marengo, IA when my husband was stationed in Korea. It was all such a long time ago it sometimes seems like a dream.

Going back to the Czech Republic last year (2000) stirred up a lot of emotions and feelings; where I was born, our old homes and my father's business looked like time had stood still all those years".

I only wish my parents would have lived to see the Berlin wall come down and to see a free Czech Republic flag fly over their old homeland. Our early years in the United States of America taught un humility, patience, perseverance, and appreciation. I have documented it all and have pictures of where we came from, for the sake of my two surviving children, and for American, Czech, and Check/American History". She said.

Mrs. Newman married a fellow Czech refugee after graduation from Amana High School, Amana, Iowa in 1956. Her husband, the late LTC Frank Charles Newman, US Army, was killed in Vietnam five days before he was scheduled to rotate from his second tour of duty.

LTC Newman was a highly decorated Army Aviation Commander, and one of only a few Czech refugees to serve in Southeast Asia and Vietnam.

Other tragedies in Mrs. Newman's life include having to bury three sons, (one who was killed by a drunk driver), being afflicted with cancer, and being stuck speechless for over a year. Despite all the tragedies and adversities in her life, Eva Honolka Newman's positive and vivacious spirit prevails.

Mrs. Newman was a guest and guest speaker for the Czech Air Force and Czech dignitaries in Prague on April 27th, 1995 for the commemoration of the 50th Anniversary of VE day. Ceremonies included dedication of a permanent display, at the museum, of LTC Newman's uniforms, medals, photos, and military memorabilia.

As a patriotic guest speaker. Mrs. Newman shares her inspiring real-life story of tragedy triumph, and deep faith, with audiences of all sizes, including civic organizations, schools, churches, business organizations, and military units. She is regularly the keynote speaker for Alabama Girls State, Alabama Boys State, and the Hugh O'Brien Foundation.

Mrs. Newman was awarded the prestigious Americanism Medal by the National Society, Daughters of the American Revolution (NSDAR) March 8, 1994. It is the highest honor given to a Naturalized American Citizen buy the DAR. She was the eight recipients in 104 years,

Mrs. Newman is Supervisor of State Capital Receptionist for the State of Alabama, and makes her home in Montgomery, Alabama,

2002 Voting Experience Unveiled at Village

Shelby County Reporter, Columbiana, Alabama, April 3, 2002
By: Perry Pearson, Reporter Staff Writer

The American Village and Montevallo unveiled its newest edition on Monday – The Alabama Power Voting Experience

The Voting Experience located in the Village's historic Colonial Courthouse, traces the history of the right to vote from the bridge in Lexington VA during the American Revolution to a Czechoslovakian immigrant's tireless work to encourage Americans to not take for granite political freedoms many across the world though without

The interactive shrine to advocates and milestones in voting rights include former presidents John Adams and Andrew Jackson, 19th century civil rights leader Frederick Douglass, and the women's suffrage leader Susan B Anthony

The exhibit also features three Alabamians who in the latter part of the 20th century made their own mark on voting rights.

John Lewis, a U.S. Congressman from Georgia he was born in Troy, led a 1965 march from Selma to Montgomery across the Edmund Pettus Bridge as marchers were attacked with clubs and tear gas. Lewis strife helped lead to the establishment of the 24th amendment to the constitution, abolishing state poll taxes, and the 1965 Voting Rights Act which outlaw's literacy test.

Vietnam War veteran John Hanson helped break down another barrier – making sure those old enough to fight and die for their country could also vote.

After the Tuscaloosa resident was drafted in at the age of 20, he urged members of Congress to pass the 26th amendment which lowered the voting age to 18.

"Now that the hurdles of race, sex and age have been jumped," interpreter Sam Barnett said, as a light appeared on a portrait of the Montgomery woman, Eva Honolka Newman.

In 1951 when she was 16 Newman's family escaped to America from Communist Czechoslovakia fleeing religious and political persecution.

Her earliest memories include near her home by the Nazis during World War Two and later occupation by Stalin Soviet regime. Her family was imprisoned and separated for a time.

Newman who serves as the supervisor of capital receptionists in Montgomery also survived the loss of four sons a husband killed in Vietnam and cancer, but narrator says she loves her adopted country.

Newman who was on hand for the exhibit unveiling is a frequent public speaker across the state willing to tell her story for free to any group who listen.

"Ask yourselves, how many times have you failed to exercise your right to vote. Voting every time there is an election, this is a crying need of America.

"When we vote, we help America fulfill her destiny," a recording said during the exhibit.

Tom Walker executive director of The Village thanked Alabama power for their $50,000 donation towards the Voting Experience project.

"So many young people will be touched by this exhibit," Walker said. "We are seeing 45,000 students a year, and we are having to turn school groups away.

Walker also thanked several local and state representatives for their help, many of whom were in attendance.

Walker also announced The Village will be one of 12 Alabama attractions to be featured on a new postal stamp.

Alabama power CEO Charles McHenry said the company proudly participated in helping to develop the Voting Experience.

"One mantra of Alabama Power is to participate in the community and the state," he said. We all must participate in government and one way is to vote.

Newman said she was "overwhelmed" to be one of the eight Americans featured.

"I felt like all the trials and tribulations I have gone through to arrive at this destination and this place were meant to be," she said.

2002 Czech Native Knows Value and Cost of Freedom

The Montgomery Standard – Friday, July 5, 2002
By: Katie Krew, Contributing Writer

Eva Newman is a Patriot, in America in the deepest sense of the word the fact that she was born in Trutnov, Czechoslovakia 65 years ago only strengthens her reference for the one thing so many Americans take for granted - freedom.

She knows what it is like to run scared from a government that controls and owns everything, down to one's thoughts. She knows what it is like having hunger and thirst that are never quenched. She knows what it is like to have sleepless nights spent in a crowded cell with 500 other women and children and swarms of lice, fleas, and ticks so thick that they form a living wallpaper.

She knows what it is like to lose her Homeland, her language and her culture and come to a new place that promises nothing but offers a chance.

Eva Newman has a message, and it comes at a time when many Americans need to be reminded of our country's roots.

Coming to America

Newman and her parents, sister and three brothers arrived in New Orleans April 26, 1951 - a date Newman will never forget because her father died 32 years later to the day. Getting off the boat, the refugees were herded like cattle and sorted by assigned to states. They were going to Iowa, and Newman was only sure of one thing.

"We came broken, we came hungry, we came torn and we came scared," she said. It really was not the promise of anything, but there was the promise of opportunity to pursue happiness with hope.

Hard work, determination and plenty of patience began to pay off for the family, and before long Newman's father struck a deal with a man trying to sell a failing bakery. Within five years the business was booming.

It was during this time of blossoming that Newman's parents located a young man that they had met long ago in the camps - a man that they made a bargain with when their eldest daughter Eva was just a child of 11, and he was 21.

"I had a pre-arranged marriage by my parents" Newman said. I could not sail off into the sunset madly in love.

Could It Be love?

Frank Charles Newman was a highly educated man, a native of Czechoslovakia, who escaped by joining the United States Army. He could read, write, and speak six languages. He was steadily working himself through the ranks of the US military, and by the time Newman's family invited him to come for a visit one Christmas when she was 18, he was a second Lieutenant.

He returned on April Fool's day with a small box containing an engagement ring and a wedding band. Newman thought it was a joke, but three months later July 4, 1957, her father put her on a plane to meet her bridegroom in Austin TX.

"He slept on the couch for the next three months and he only dated me," Newman said. "I thought married life was the most wonderful thing invented. I did not have to cook because he took me out every night. He tried to teach me how to bowl and how to drive a car, and we went to the movies a lot.

Newman was falling in love with a gentle "gentleman and a scholar", something she was not even aware of until he came home one day with the news he was being sent to Korea.

By the time he left, Newman found out she was pregnant. She gave birth alone and she buried her first son alone.

The family was living in Ozark, AL when Newman's husband was sent to Vietnam. He fought in the first tour and was sent again for the second. It was during the second tour, five days before his scheduled return that he was killed in a plane crash on February 24, 1970.

At the time of his death LTC, a master aviator with more than 4,500 flying hours who was qualified to fly 26 aircrafts. For his service to the country, he earned the Legion of Merit, the nation's second highest award, as a as well as the Distinguished Flying Cross, the Bronze Star Metal, the Purple Heart, and the Air Metal with 22 Oak leaf Cup custom clusters

"Frank would have done anything for freedom he believed anytime you cannot develop yourself as a human being, it usually means there is some kind of oppression somewhere that doesn't allow you to come to the fullest potential you are capable of" she said. "Having studied all the great philosophers like Plato, he was well versed an understood what freedom is. He wanted it for everybody, not just himself. It was his passion."

And as a bereaved widow, it was that passion that gave her strength and a focus.

"When the soldiers folded the United States flag on his casket into a triangle and they handed it to me, I laid my hand on Frank's casket and I said "You were willing to serve and die for this country and Liberty, and I promise I am willing to live and serve this country and Liberty. It is a promise I made, and at this point in my life, I am really saturated with it. I am red, white, and blue from my head down to my toes.

In addition to sharing her story with various groups she is an active spokesperson for the American village in Montevallo, a civic Education Center with a mission to strengthen and renew the foundations of American citizenship.

Her portrait now hangs in the Village's Colonial Courthouse as part of the Alabama Power Voting Experience, along with famous voting advocates from long ago such as the 19th century civil rights leader Frederick Douglas and the women's suffrage leader Susan B Anthony. Newman was chosen as one of three Alabamians who have made a mark on voting rights in the 20th century.

"We take a lot for granite, but the time is here when taking the shortcut and looking the other way is not acceptable. Ask yourself, citizens, how many times have you failed to exercise your right to vote? Voting every time there is an election - this is the crying need of America." Newman's recorded voice says at the exhibit.

Newman knows firsthand what happens when citizens of a democracy choose not to vote, and their complacency allows an intruder to take charge. That is precisely what happened to her homeland in 1948.

When human visit schools she tells her story, she reaches out to America's disinterested youth by appealing to their imaginations, trying to make them understand what they have.

"Those who criticize democracy just don't have any real conception of the alternative. Culture, memory itself, is a condition of freedom," she said. Under totalitarianism you only have pseudo-culture. The entire country wears headphones, hearing one voice. A dictatorship is total isolation cultural, intellectual and moral."

Newman's passion continues to flow when she sponsors soldiers from the Czech Republic who come to study at Maxwell Air Force Base in Montgomery, Alabama.

"One of the first things I tried to project to them, next to the Declaration of Independence, the Constitution and the Bill of Rights, so they understand the foundations of this nation by the founding fathers, is that the Biblical principles, which is hard for them because they were raised agonistic," Newman said.

But to Newman, these young soldiers from her native land are not the only ones floundering without religion.

We as a nation have gotten less spiritual than we used to be. We need that spirituality because that is part of morality." she said. When people tell you that the Ten Commandments offended them, you must ask yourself, If Eva Newman could make a law and she would say for you to have a good life, you cannot kill" - would that offend you? Even if they were not commandments from God just ten laws, you would have to agree they have value."

And now Newman - a woman who lost a husband and four sons and survived cancer - wants to share one more lesson.

"I know about the stage where you feel alone, but now I am at the stage to help humanity see that they we are not human beings living a spiritual experience but spiritual beings having a human experience" she said. "Jesus Christ left us His Spirit. It is within us, and if we can develop that spirituality and embrace it in such a way, we will realize we can have a better life.

2003 The United States of the Offended

Displaying the Ten Commandments – August 12, 2003
Where are we headed, America?

No prayers school – No mention of God during graduation, and Heaven forbid, at a ball game. Should the Pledge of Allegiance be scrapped? Should "under God" be removed.

Now, to some people, the motto of our nation is offensive and so are the 10 Commandments. The dollar bill bears the words "In God we Trust"; to some that is a farce. Some people claim that life before birth is not life. Some even believe the government can function without the moral foundation of the Holy Scriptures of the Law of God.

In an act of intolerance, signs that say "Proud to be an American" have been removed to not offend certain people. To be offended seems to be our new bright right. Is being grateful, helpful, and a believer a negative? It seems some do not understand nor respect the structure of our government; to how can we protect our system of ordered Liberty elected by our Founding Fathers?

"The American way" has been developed through struggle, trials, and victories; by the men and women who have sought freedom. Our soldiers, sailors, airmen, and marines fought and died at places like Pearl Harbor, Bataan, New Guinea, Iwo Jima, and the South Pacific, North Africa, Europe. Asia Korea, Vietnam and Southeast Asia, the Persian Gulf, Afghanistan, and Iraq, and far too many places to mention; some places around the World I cannot even pronounce.

From 1938 to 1945 our family lived under the oppression of Hitler's regime, in Czechoslovakia. We were told that nobody had ever seen God, so why we believe in a fairy tale? Churches were locked, bibles were burned, mother government would "take care of you if you" had blonde hair, blue eyes, and the right ethnicity.

In 1948, when "we the people" could have elected democracy, we elected communism because in parentheses (again as before) mother government would take care of us in the new coop society, where everyone is equal. Again, churches were locked, and bibles were burned; nobody had ever seen God.

We were trained to have strong bodies, so we could serve the government. We were given limited information about the parliament and were not allowed to participate in government affairs, in a cool society. We were spiritually dead, like a herd of oxen, being led to the promised paradise of communism.

We escaped in 1948, after many horrifying trepidations in jails and displaced person camps. We sought refuge in the United States of America. we arrived on the shores of New Orleans in 1951; torn, broken, scarred, scared, and hungry promise of opportunity to follow happiness with hope and that is all we needed.

Our nation has a language of its own. We did not ask Americans to learn to speak Czech just because we did not speak English. We Dylan diligently followed your laws, learned your language, served in your military, and some of us paid the ultimate price for our Liberty. All of us became American citizens. With our Czech heritage in the background, we became proud Americans.

In Washington, DC we went to visit the US Supreme Court. We looked with awe at the carving of Moses holding the 10 commandments. We were humbled by the beauty of people that would adopt such laws into their lives. In the House of Representatives, we saw the model of the United States of America, "In God We Trust" engraved in stone. With sadness we recalled our past, when there was nothing to believe in except the cruelty of human beings with no moral compass, void of a higher being.

We were proud to become citizens of the United States of America. In America we could develop ourselves physically, mentally, and spiritually. Our live became blessed, productive, and we were happy again. The

Founding Fathers used biblical principles for a foundation to establish a country that we now call our home. Our founders were good Patriots but now some people are offended by the very ideals that foundation bestowed upon us.

I have never gone anywhere where people prayed in worship that I was told "I had to do that". Our parents told us that if we were going to live here, we must learn to live that way, and if we should get offended by that way of life, then we had a choice - the right to leave.

Anything that is worthy of adopting into our life's journey to make it pleasant, good, motivating, or inspiring is worth displaying. After all, paintings are, and if you do not like them, do not look at them.

God gave us the 10 Commandments. All religions have some form of commandments. They are LAWS and what better place to display them than in the courthouse? You do not have to look at them. You do not have to adopt them, but what is wrong with "Thou shall not kill"? Honor your mother and father, do not commit adultery do not steal etc.

Nobody has dictated that if we go to the Alabama Supreme Court House, we must look at and read the 10 Commandments engraved in granite there. They do not dictate any religion or church be adopted or even infer that "Church" and "State" be intertwined in any way at all. If it is wrong to display them in Alabama, then when are we going to blast away the 10 Commandments from the U. S. Supreme Court House in Washington DC.

If displaying the 10 Commandments causes resentment by flagrantly violating one's standards of what is right and decent. "God help America" to understand more fully the 10 commandments. When the ones who are offended are through complaining and griping over our Pledge, our Motto, and the 10 commandments, I dare say "take advantage" of the great American freedom – The Right to Leave.

Wake up America, we do have a Constitution, girded by the laws of the Bible. If some people are offended, which means the act of giving displeasure, let them go some other place that will give them pleasure. Let them adopt Nazism, communism or any other "ISM" and lead a happy UN offended oppression.

Each American, either native born or Naturalized alike needs to be re-dedicate themselves to the oath of citizenship. Each one teaches one and each ten teach ten, to defend the laws and principles of our spiritual foundation against all enemies; both foreign and domestic. let us just not sit on our "blessed assurance" in apathy and do nothing.

If my writing offends you, walk in my shoes for a day. I am a refugee and naturalized American citizen. My husband lost his life on his second tour in Vietnam, serving his country. I had five sons and a daughter. Four of my sons have died. Four times I have investigated the still face of my child, and by the grace of God I could accept what I did not have the power to change.

I have survived cancer and other serious illness, including malnutrition in the displaced persons camps.

Yes, I have lived, loved, and despaired, and by God's grace have survived. The United States of America is a healing salve on my life's wounds, and it is the wind beneath my wings. God bless the United States of America.

2010 ST. Wenceslaus, Welcomed Her Family

The Cedar Rapids Gazette, By: Molly Rossiter

The laughter is the first thing Eva Honolka Newman remembers most about St. Wenceslaus school and parish.

"If you see any pictures of us as children there were never any pictures of us laughing," Newman, 73, says by phone from her home in Montgomery. AL. "That to us was a big deal."

Newman will be a guest speaker at St. Wenceslaus' annual Goulash Day at p.m., Sunday. She will share stories of her childhood in Czechoslovakia during World War II before she and her parents became residents of a "displaced persons camp" for more than a year, and how Cedar Rapids and the St. Wenceslaus community welcomed her family to the United States.

"For the first 16 years of my life, the only emotion I knew was fear," Newman said. "afraid to be hungry, afraid of the bombings, afraid of losing my mom and dad."

Newman was 16 when her family came to the United States and Cedar Rapids. St. Wenceslaus was the first school she and her siblings attended as refugees.

"I came to St. Wenceslaus school and was so overwhelmed by the graciousness of the people", she said. "It was so unusual to be in a situation like we'd been in (at the camp) and suddenly you come to someplace like St. Wenceslaus. It is like you finally realize, "Hey, I have a soul and I'm allowed to have feelings and it's OK to laugh."

Newman now spends her time sharing her story in hopes that she can educate people about the importance of freedom and standing up for what they want.

"Right now, I see the handwriting on the wall for our nation." She said. "Religion is being ridiculed and people are wanting handouts from the government. We the people need to have the say-so of how we want our government to be."

2015 Cross of Merit

Wednesday, August 19, 2015
Embassy of the Czech Republic
Washington, D. C.

Eva Honolka Newman was awarded with the Cross of Merit of the Czech Minister of Defense, 3rd Class, for her significant merit in the development of the Ministry of Defense of the Czech Republic on August 19, 2015. Brigadier. General. Jiri Verner, Defense, Military and Air Attaché of the Czech Republic, decorated Mrs. Newman at a ceremony held at the Maxwell Air Force Base in Alabama.

Her daughter Julie, son Michael and his wife, Brigadier General Chris "Boots" Coffelt, commander of the Air War College, Col. Michael Peterson, head of the International Officers School, as well as current Czech students Col. Cepelka and Major Josef Korinek were present for the ceremony.

Eva Honolka Newman was born on May 14, 1937, in the town of Trutnov, then Czechoslovakia.

In February 1948, the communists seized power, and in 1949, the family decided to leave for exile. After a long and painful journey, they found a new home in the United States.

Eva recalls: "We arrived hungry, torn and scared, but there was a promise of opportunity to follow happiness with hope, to have the dignity of work, to praise our God, to have the freedom to love our fellow human beings, to be of service and to appreciate life as it was given to us by a power beyond ourselves."

The family settled down in Cedar Rapids, Iowa. Later, Eva married Frantisek Newman, who served as a U.S. Army pilot at Garris Air Force Base in Texas. He spoke 6 languages fluently. During his service, he was sent for an 18-month tour to Korea and then Vietnam. Five days before his scheduled return from his second tour of duty in Vietnam, LTC Frank Charles Newman died in combat on February 24, 1970.

Widowed with three small children, Eva decided to apply for a job with the U. S. Government. She took part in a selection process in Montgomery, AL, and was chosen from among 2,000 applicants to work in the U. S. Capitol.

Although she did not have a relevant educational background, she loved history and started to give public lectures. Later, she lectured on American history. Auburn University in Alabama honored her for her achievements.

In 1988, she started sponsoring foreign students, particularly those studying at the Air War College in Montgomery, Alabama. She also sponsored Czech military students from 1992 until 2005 and continues to maintain unofficial ties with the alumni.

In 1995, she received a medal for promotion of the United States of America as the eight non-American. The medal has been awarded since 1895.

2016 Sharing the Heart of Europe

Maxwell Air Force Base, Published January 5
By Airman 1ˢᵗ Class Alexa Culbert, 42ⁿᵈ Air Base Wing Public Affairs
WATCH Live interview at https://youtu.be/LOcYWZKXC-w

Eva Newman, started at the White House Confederacy in 1984 as a receptionist, poses in front of the White House of Confederacy while working at the museum MontogomeryAlabama. Newman became fascinated with the history of the house and its role in the Civil War and began working there to share its history with others.

Guest gather around First White House of Confederacy receptionist, Eva Newman as she tells stories of the house. Her bright blue eyes light up witht excitement at the chance to share her knowledge of the house and its role in the Civil War. She wears a bright welcoming smile and her patriotism shines through as she speaks, however, a strong accent suggest that she once hailed from another country. Newman loves to America's story, but she too has a story of her own to tell. Her journey began 78 years ago in the Czech Republic.

In 1937, Newman was born in Czech Republic during the occupation of Nazi forces.

I had a childhood, but the only emotion I had was fear," said Newman. "I was afraid to go to school because of the bombings, afraid of going hungry and afraid that my father would be arrested for something."

In 1948, her father made the decision for the family to escape the country and made their way across the boarder into Austria, but the authorities quickly caught up with them.

Her father was taken with the other men to become re-educated while her mother and her siblings were locked away in a large cell with 500 other women and children. After three months of being in an insect infested cell with little food, all 500 prisoners were rounded up and taken downstairs where they were ordered to remove their clothing.

Spigots were lowered down and all the women slammed theirbodies against the floor to sheild the children from what they believed to be gas, but it was only water.

During one shower, the gate behind them didn't click. At the young age of 12, Newman was ordered by her mother to squeeze through the gate opening and retrieve her clothes. Her mother and siblings followed and they made their way through an empty hallway with a door waiting for them at the end.

They punched through the door not knowing if it would lead then to freedom or right back into captivity. They landed in the middle of downtown Budapest and hurriedly made their way to the train station.

After begging for passage on a train, they ended in Vienna, Aistria where they reunited with her Father.

They were then put into a deportation camp and awaited approval to immigrate to America. After two and a half years permission was granted, and they imigrated to the United States.

In 1951, the family arrived in New Orleans and relocated to Iowa to begin a new life, where her father eventually opened a bakery.

After high school graduation, Newman wanted to further her education at the Art Instiue in Chicago, however, her father had another idea.

In 1957, at 18 years old, she was put on a plane to Austin, Texas with nothing but a wedding dress and $5 in her pocket, to meet the man she was arranged to marry.

Waiting for her at the airport was a man that her father met while in an Austrian displacement camp, named Frank Newman.

They were married immediately. After two months of being married, Frank, who just enlisted into the United States Army, was called to serve 18 months in Korea.

"He said, Eva I have tot ake you back to live with your parents. I have to go to Korea, and I don't want you here in Texas alone," said Eva. "Istarted crying, I don't want to go home. I'll have to work in the bakery again."

When he returned, the couple began their military life, moving from basee-to-base. Over the next six years, Frank and Eva became the parents of three children, life was good for the Newman fmaily.

However, in 1970, the family was ripped apart by the death of Frank while serving in the Vietnam War.

Frank Newman's last assignment was at the International School as the Czech Republic advisor at Maxwell Air Force Base. After he passed, Eva decided to stay in Montgomery and raise her children. She felt like she needed to learn more about the history in her new home in the South, so she beguan volunteering at the White House of Confederacy.

When Frank died, I absolutely had to influence the young people about patriotiam and the honor of it in our flag and what it means to us as a nation," she said. "That's what I started doing (then) and that is what I do to this day.

One day while working at the White House of Confederacy, Eva was surrised to see a Czech Republic Officer walk in who was attending Air University at Maxwell Air Force Base.

"I never believed that day would come that I would have Czech Republic officers walk in. Frank never got to finish what he started so I had to sponsor and teach these Czechs." Said Eva Newman.

In 2002, Newman became a Goodwill Ambassador, aprogram created by the International Officers School at Air University that supports international officers and their families while they are attending school at Maxwell. Over the next nine years she sponsored a total of 55 Czech Republic International Officer School students.

Eva Newman was cognized for her love and loyalty to her country through the work she did at IOS, however, Eva never forgot the blood and tears that went into immigrating to American and the chance of a new life that it gave her.

"She has earned the right to become an American, she really gives you a sense of patriotiam, when you think of someone who is from a different county and is more patriotic than you, it really stirs you up inside," said Henry Howard, White House of Cenfederacy tour guide.

Newman's love and pride for her country shows through to the people she meets and reminds others what it means to be a good American.

"We gave everything, our heritage and our language for an intangible called freedom, and it is my upmost obligation to give until my last breath to a nation that so graciously adopted us, said Newman.

???? Montgomery Woman Speaks to Local DAR

Hoover/Vestavia Neighborhood Paper
By: Judy Halse, News Staff Writer

Eva Honolka Newman of Montgomery, Alabama shared a love story between her and America at a luncheon held at the Country Club of Birmingham, Alabama.

Speaking to the Princess Sehoy Chapter of the Daughters of the American Revolution, she brought tears to many during her talk.

Before becoming a United States citizen, the Czechoslovakia native and her family escaped from a World War II Nazi prison camp, she said, describing the depravities she suffered in prison.

"My only emotion was fear," the petite woman recalled. "I never went to church until I was 14, but my parents hid a Bibleand a radio that the Nazi officers were always looking for.

"Church bells rang when the war was over, and we could go and worship our Creator, how wonderful it was."

"Those who don't understand our Unted States liberty, certainly can't understand how to defend it," she said.

She later lost a husband and son in Vietnam. He husbanmd, the late LTC Frank C. Newman, a fellow Czech refugee, was killed in a 1970 plane crash, leaving her to raise three small children. She eventually triumphed over cancer and loss of several sons, but it has not embittered her.

She revels in her life in America and the activities of her son and daughters, she said.

Mrs. Newman is only the ight recepipent of the prestigious Americanism Medal awarded in the 114-year history of the National Society of the Daugthers of the American Revolution. She received hers last year at the state conference, which cited her for the inspirational and motivational speeches she has given to hundreds of schools, businesses, churches and civic organizations.Mrs. Newman is now supervisor of Capital receptionists with the State of Alabama.

Flag Is Her Call to Duty

Frances King, Correspondent

She was 16 years old, hungry, torn, poor and scared when she set foot on American soil with her family as a Czechoslovakian refugee.

I had no promise of anything but an opportunity to pursue happiness with a hope and a chance to be free." Eva H. Newman told members and guests of the LaFayette Stuidy Club last Thursday.

Since becoming a naturalized American citizen, Mrs. Newman, who won the prestigious NSDAR Americanism Award last spring, has told her story of tragedy and triumph to audiences across the county proudly and chides American-boarn citizens who use the flag-raising time at athletic events to get refreshments or talk. She carries with her the triangylar-folded American flag that draped the casket of her husband, United States Army LTC Frank Charles Newman, killed on his second tour of duty in Vietnam.

Mrs. Newman says the flag is a "diploma", a call to duty. If my husband could die for this country, I have an obligation to live for this country."

The story Mrs. Newman tells is one of almost continuous adversity that could have ended in despair. "I have survived because of prayer and the love of Jesus." She says.

Mrs. Newman, her parents, two brothers and her sister escaped from their hiomeland, Trutnov, Czechoslovakia, when she was 11 years old. Following World War II her father, who own a bakery with 25. Em[ployees, was accused of conspiracy by the new communist government, when he refused to be "re-edicated."

World War II, was over and the government had control of a co-op society. My father was told he was a capitalist. He walked into his bakery one day and someone else was seated behind his desk. They told him he ownded too much.

"When the government tends toward collectivism and plays the role of a helping hand, it eventually owns you," she said.

John Honolka's entire family fled the country but were caught, handcuffed and incarcerated in Budapest, Hungary. Eva, along with her mother, sister and brothers, spent six months in a cell housing some 500 women and children. The prison was infested with fleaqs and ticks and had one bathroom, she said.

Herded to the basement for showers, Eva's family feared they were going to the gas chamber. "To this day. I fear stepping inside an elevator." She said. Infants who died in the prison were hauled out in paper sacks.

During one of their trips to the shower, when no guards were around, Mrs. Honolka seized the opportunity and walked out of the prison with her four children, to catch a train to Austria. When passports were checked and Mrs. Honolka had none, she begged the guards on her knees, "Please, in the name of God, don't make us go back."

The guards had mercy on the mother and chilren and they got off the train in Vienna. They found refuge in a displaced persons camp and spent the next 3 ½ years in such camps under deplorable conditions. Two blankets hung by ropes in a corner served as partitions for their room. Mr. Honolka remained imprisoned in Hungry.

After Mr. Honolka's release, the family was reunited with the help of the American Red Cross. They sailed to the United States, landing in New Orleans, Louisana, with nothing but their hopes of a better life.

Mr. Honolka became a naturalized American citizen, opend a bakery with two ovens and expanded until he was shipping baked goods in 18 trucks. He invented and marketed the polyethylene bread bag, which replaced paper sacks for stroage of bread loaves, said Mrs. Newman.

Her parents lived in the country until their deaths, Mr. Honolka's in 1983 and Mrs. Honolka in 1987.

Mrs. Newman's husband was also a Czech refugee and immigrant. Newman rose from the United States Army private to the rank of LTC. He bcame a highly decorated master aviator and Army Aviation Unit Commander. LTC Newman was scheduled to go home in five days when he was killed at Phu Bia, Vietnam.

"When my husband died I was left in Ozark, Albama, with three small children. I took his wings and pinned them on my sons' chests." Said Mrs. Newman

Ten years later, the American flag that draped his casket would draped the casket of her second son, "Steve Allen "Chip" Newman, killed by a drunken driver of Flag Day, his brother Michael's 21st birthday.

Upon leaving that morning for a day at the beach, 17-year-old Chip rushed back into the house to hang out the Statrs and Stripes. The last words his mother heard him say were, "Mom, I forgot to hang out the flag today." At 5:45 p.m. State Troopers appeared on Mrs. Newman's doorstep with the news of his death.

That day, Mrs. Newman said, she stayed on her knees praying for so long that she couldn't walk when she got up. "But as devasted as I was, I was proud to be an American."

Today, she is grateful for the freedom to practice her Christian faith, the privilege to pray and take her son's casket into a achurch for his funeral-freedoms taken for granted by many Americans, but unavailable in some countries.

She is deeply troubled about the erosion of such freedoms. "I do not get involved in the big-time government; I'm not that smart," Mrs. Newman said following the meeting, "If I knew all the answers I would be in Wshington, D.C. But I know enough to know that if people demand the government take care of them, they are giving up their liberty," she said.

"Liberty doesn't erode overnight. Its like the mustard seed Jesus mentioned in the Bible. It was so small you couldn't see it. It's the same with liberty and freedom. It is lost in little seeds, one at a time."

Mrs. Newman know first hand "what animals people can become when the spirtual dimension is taken away." She said in her speech. "For the first 14 years of my life it was totally alien to me."

Restoring prayer to public schools is vital for children to develop spiritually as well as physically and mentally, Mrs. Newman believes. "We are giving young people the wrong message. As adults we perform the rituals of praying before congressional sessions in Washington. Yet, we say, if we did that in class, someone might be offended."

"We need to balance that out. We have to allow that same priviege for our children even if we do offend. The creator of our nation is also the creator of the world."

As freedom erodes, Mrs. Newman fears Americans may eventually lose every vestige of public prayer and acknowledgment of God'in public life. "I am more conscious of losing freedom because I have lived under other systems. I am forever on watch for someone to take it away. It is my magnifienct obsess."

Her obsession is not easy to quell. Stricken with cancer of the esophagus several years ago, Mrs. Newman lost half of her windpipe to surgery, leaving her unable to speak above a whisper. Physicians told her she would never egain her voice.

"In a year-and-a-half I got my voice back. The doctor said he had never seen anything like it. It was because of my will to rise above circumstances and determination to allow God to shape my life. I believe each life has a plan."

God's plan for her, speaking on patriotiam and freedom, has been confirmed through her "red, white and blue dates." She said. Mrs.

Newman was married on July 4. Her son Michael was born on Flad Day, also Sunday and Father's Day. Her son Steven died on Flag Day.

Three years ago Mrs. Newman decided it was time to stop taking speaking engagments. "On the 27th of May, Mike calded and said "Good Morning Grandman." It was Memorail Day. Another grandchild is on the way, "My daughter is also expecting she said, the due date is June 14.""

Mrs. Newman's personal story has been told to churches, schools, civic groups and militay groups

In 1993 she traveled over 3,000 miles and spoke 60 times, all in her free time. She is supervisor of the Capital Receptionists with the State of Alabama in Montogery. In addition, she sponsors international Officer students, primarily for the Czech and Slovak Republics, who come to Maxwell AFB, and a hostof other visitors to this country.

Mrs. Newman says her motivation is a divine calling to "go and tell that Jesus Christ is Lord and talk about freedom. It's not easy, because I have feelings. But if I ever get to the point of not feeling, I will quit…"

"It is my way of paying back the nation that so graciouslt adopted us" she says. "Those of us who have lived with out freedom, liberty and justice, treasure them dearly in our hearts and soul.

JOHN AND JARMILA'S CORRESPONDENCE TO FAMILY IN GERMANY

9 October 1948

Dear Parents, (Joseph and Berta Honolka)

TODAY I AM WRITING YOU this letter in hopes that you can help me.

The situation in Trutnov has forced us to flee on the 15ᵗʰ of September. I had been put in jail for political reasons, so I decided to flee with my family via Kaschau, Hungary and Budapest to Austria. Our driver was not reliable, so we fell into the hands of the police. We have been in prison for 14 days in Szombathely, Hungry, and in Budapest. Another trial is waiting us. We have not given up hope and ask you to arrange our immigration permit for us. If this would be possible, we could hopefully become free.

It would be awful to have to return to Czechoslovakia, that would be the end. We have had a lot to suffer, our situation is very grave.

Fast help is necessary. Here is the messenger information:

> John Honolka born 12-25-1905, currently living in Trutnov.
> Jarmila Honolka (Kralik), born 7-26-1920 currently living in Trutnov.
> Adelbert (Oldrich) Kralik, born 12-12-1909.
> Children: Eva, Vladimir (Don), Vlasta (Patricia) and Hans John.

It is all too tragic to believe. If you can help me then please, quickly. We will never be a burden to you, I just want to get out of here. Reply to this address, John Honolka, Budapest, Moson Yinten, Tolinshaus.

My greeting to you, perhaps for the last time. Hans

14 June 1949

Dear Sister (Helene),

We received your last letter. Honzik (John) really likes it here. On the 3rd and 4th. we were in Tuttlingen, Germany to get shots. Now Honzik (John) has a high fewer and lost weight. Also, we moved to a different barracks, we have a larger room, it is easier. I received a letter from New York City regarding our moving to the United States of America. If things do not work out with Norway I will stay here for a while, then immigrate to the United States of America.

Last week I was in Ludwigshafen, Stuttgart, Ulm and Friedrichshafen, Germany. Got a lot accomplished. I am going to wait 14 days, then I let you know about vacation.

The weather is better now, but we had a lot of rain. The water in the lake is warm, it is great for swimming, the children have a nice tan.

Honzik (John) tells everyone that Helene has gone in a large railroad car. We have not heard anything from Trutnov.

We received the package from Mother. It had a head pillow for Honzik (John). Lada (Don) received an invitation from Switzerland again, also she got a package with chocolate and condensed milk.

It is ok here, but I wish I had something to do. I also received a card from H. Prelat, he does not seem to realize what goes on in the world, everything is probably going to come to a head by next year, but not much is known or written about it.

You can all hope to get back home, just wait and see. Should we suddenly go, I will write right away so you know.

All the best from all of us, also Honzik (John Jr.).

Hans (John Honolka, Sr.)

30 June 1949

Dear Mom,

I received your card, I was convinced that I had written you, meanwhile I wrote to Willie. The package arrived in good condition. Honzik received his head cushion (could possibly be a pillow), he does remember grandmother well. We were pleased about the shoes from father and your delicious cake.

The children are now outside in fresh air all day, and in the afternoon, they are by the lake and eat three times as much as at they did at home. Today I could use my stockpile that I left at home, now they also must eat dry bread. Everyone is tanned and Honzik has also recovered. We were in Tuttlingen, Germany 4 weeks ago for a medical examination where he received shots. A week later he got a high fever and was bedridden for three days.

Monday Helene will come to us and spend her vacation here, for 14 days. Hopefully, everything will go well, and we do not have to leave suddenly. We are very curious where we will end up. From Stuttgart, Germany we will travel by airplane to Oslo, Norway. Already received a message from there that they are preparing everything for us.

Altogether, a total of 152 Czech is accepted by Norway, from all camps. 45 from Lindau, Germany and the first 6 are already gone. 12 will returned to the CSR (Czech Socialist Republic) as partisans, they are will be well equipped and paid. However, if they get caught, they will hang. Surely, you are following the events in the CSR in "Die Neue Zeitung" (The New Newspaper). It will all be short lived. Everything will be over in 1951.

We have received a message from Milek Kralik is still doing some business, but it is very weak, in Trutnov there is an exhibit in the converted Faltis factory (linen manufacturer and a cotton weaving mill).

Oldrich Kralik was sentenced to two years in prison for simply trying to cross the border. We did not know that he was already in Salzburg, Germany. He is in Trutnov.

Couldn't you come to us next Sunday with the discounted return ticket? It is a good connection with express train? The train arrives is at half past eleven in Lindau and you could go back Monday morning? Inform yourself and if possible, come.

30 June 1949

Dear Grandmother and Grandfather,

First, I want to thank you for all the good things you have sent us. It is always well received. Often, your shipments have helped us in our bad situation. Maybe, later, we will have a chance to pay you back for everything. Please stay healthy.

Please, everyone stays healthy, so that we can all meet happily in Trutnov. If you can, please come and visit us. It would make us all happy, especially it would make the children happy.

Eva often asks about you and Deda (Grandfather). Also, Lada (Don) and Vlasta (Patricia) think of you and talk about how nice it was when we all lived together in Trutnov.

Next week Helene is coming to us, so please if you can, come also.

Before we leave, I will write another letter. Honzik (Jon, Sr.) and the children go swimming at Bodensee (Lake Constance). He speaks German very well but mixes Czech with it, which is a lot of fun. Warm greeting to you both,

Your Jarmila

28 December 1949

Dear Parents, Lindau,

On Tuesday the 27th of December, we received a nice Christmas package from Willie. Lada (Don) also received a package from his foster parents in Switzerland. He got a nice sweater, chocolate, 4 games, Nescafe and cookies, candies, dates, figs, etc.

On the 23rd of December. I received papers from the French for Lada (Don) to move to Switzerland. We waited for two months, now Lada can go at the end of January for 3 months to Rapperswill, Switzerland. I also got the Visa for Switzerland. On the 27th I went with Lada to the French police in Lindau to get the papers. It cost 32 DM for the passport. Helene's Weinachtsgeschenk (Christmas gift) went to it.

We had a nice Christmas, are satisfied, but without your help it would not be that way. We had a small tree, bought Feather boxes(?) and school supplies for the kids. Honzik (John) got a wooden train, Vlasta (Patricia) got coloring books and color pencils. The best gift was from Helene, the money was very appreciated.

On Sunday we had a gift giving for the children in the camp. Had a large tree with electric lights in the mess hall. Each child received a large sack (kg.) with nuts, figs, dates, chocolates, mandarin oranges, cookies, and a few textile things. Honzik and Vlasta also received a small metal wagon and a Nilschaus.

Eva got bacon, meat fat and milk. Christmas, we had potato salad and sausages. Two pigs were slaughtered in camp, we had pork both Holidays. We were also photographed. Jamila was sad; she was probably homesick. Eva has a lot of friends here; she goes to school with them. There were singing in a Christmas program. I let you know in the New Year if I can get to Norway.

Mr. Beier sent a package with pfeffernusse cookies and wafers. We were happy about that. We have not received the clothes we were promised.

Right now, the weather is nice, only the Alps remind us it is winter.

If Father could send me some money to get Lada's (Don's) passport I would really appreciate it. I also must pay for the ticket to Konstanz, Switzerland. Will send some Cigarettes and soap to you.

Thank Willie for the package, also Helene. I wish you all the best for the New Year, especially health.

Hope all will go well, 1950 will be the year to decide the future. Hans

29 March 1950

Dear Mom,

I want to write you in detail today to answer your last letter. We are also deeply sorry and sometimes we cannot believe that father is no longer with us. But our worries leave us little time to think about it.

But often we look at the photos in which father looks so naturally. I am glad that I got to see him again alive in the hospital and that I could also accompany him on his last journey. In my thoughts I am often in your stuebel (living room) and at the cemetery there. If you move to Holzheim, Germany you will also be able to move on, in any case it is no longer necessary that you do not work so hard anymore. Everything is already set up so that you should have peace now. and if possible, come to us in the summer. Now, we have very warm spring weather, only the Austrian and Swiss Alps are still covered in snow.

Sunday, I took Lada (Don) to Constance, by ship and at the border to Kreuzlingen (a town in NE Switzerland), family Oswald and Berta Wanners (Wameln) from Rapperswill, St. Gallen, Switzerland was waiting for us.

The customs controls, on either side, were quickly over and we were well catered on the Swiss side. (Honzik was also there), we got chocolate, ham sandwiches and Nescafe for our way back and then we said goodbye to Lada (Don) and the Swiss and Lada (Don) drove with them via Winterthur in Zurich to his new home. Now I am waiting for Eva's visa, she is invited to visit to the canton of Graubunden (Alpine Children's Home Malix) in Switzerland, she is now also on vacation.

I now must tell you that our family has grown, March 14, 1950, Tomas is a beautiful boy, particularly good like Vlasta (Patricia) was, happy and healthy. Jarmila is back home. Another room was added, while Jarmila was in the hospital, I painted and furnished everything. Now we have lots of space and live comfortably. We received beautiful baby clothes from Switzerland, Norway, and Luxembourg, we now have plenty.

Most likely we will receive a (new) stroller from our camp management. There are four packages on the way from the United States.

14 days ago, I also applied to an employment ad, in my specialty with a company in Ecuador (Central America). They are looking for a specialist in Quito, Ecuador. I sent copies of report cards, the conditions are particularly good. A furnished villa is available and 3000 cruzeiro (circa 400 DM). They speak Spanish there. I wrote in English. Australia is still open, from where we receive good news. United States is also still waiting. I have not heard anything else from Norway. I do not have enough money for correspondence, I had a lot of unexpected expenses. Jarmila had to sell some of her things, otherwise I could not even have sent Lada away. Write again soon.

Hans

12 May 1950

Dear Mother,

I received your letter with 20 DM and want to thank you for the money especially. Took the money right away to the German police to get a Visa for Eva. By the end of the month Eva will go to Switzerland.

We received a genuinely nice letter from Lada's (Don's) foster parents. They like for Lada to stay and they will get his vacation extended. Hope all gets approved and he can stay. He goes to school there.

Vlasta (Patricia) could also go but right now I do not have the means to make it happen. It takes a lot of documents and things to get it done. Honzik (John) is outside the whole day and little Tonik (Tom) is nice and gives us a lot of fun. In camp we have a lot of Polish, whole families came. In the meadow between the camp and the street we had Circus Krone for 3 days. A big circus, the children went with Jarmila.

We do not hear anything from Trutnov, Czech Republic, we do not have any idea what is happening there.

The weather is nice here, we have lots of people by the sea and in Lindau they opened a new Play Casino.

We look at the pictures of Father often and are sad. It is nice that you have Willie close and that you will move closer. You said you will move on the 1st of June. In June there is a get together for the Sudetenland German's, they think 60,000 will show in Kempten, Germany.

How are things with Willie (Wilhelm Honolke), did he lose his job and is he already in touch with the United States of America? How is

Hildegard and her parents, etc. Hope to hear again from you soon, best wishes from Jarmila and Children.

Hans

PS. Could I get a large empty sturdy box from you or Willie. I cannot find one here, need one as a suitcase.

24 May 1950

Dear Mother,

At the beginning of this letter, I must apologize that I did not write to you by the 8th of May and for Mother's Day. We talk a lot about you and Father, but a lot of things came up with kids. Please do not be mad that we forgot.

Eva turned 13 on the 14th of May, we could not do anything special for her. Wednesday of last week I went with a child from camp to Munich. The child was admitted to the University Hospital for an operation. Since I was done by 11 AM I went to visit Lene. (Helene). Was there for 2 hours, had a nice visit. At 7 PM I went back to Lindau. She told me that she was going on vacation on August 1st. She is going to come home for Pentecost, talk about it, I am sure we will still be here.

Lada (Don) sent a nice card from a trip to Lucerne, Switzerland, and the four woods town lake? I have news from Trutnov, they have taken things (bricks) away from Kralik's, gave him 10,000 Koruna. Also, they are supposed to leave their home. I think things are not going well for them, they are too old for something like that. Zdenek (Cousin to the Honolka Children, Son of Jarmila's sister) writes often to Lada (Don).

I go swimming with Vlasta (Patricia) and Honzik (John) every day at the lake. The water is nice and warm. We had big waves on Sunday, we stayed in the water till late at night.

On Pentecost, Austrian, Swiss and Germans get together with about 20 ships for races on the Bodensee. Also have big fireworks. The traffic has already picked up. We have a fast train now that comes from Hamburg and Kiel into Lindau.

Our little guy gives us a lot of pleasure, he is tanned already, he likes his food, and he is growing. (Tom)

If you come to visit with Lene (Helene) I will give you a can of ground coffee from a care package I received from the United States. We have a nice place to live with enough room.

How does Father's grave look? I am sure you go there every day. He had a nice life, now he can rest. Jarmila wants to come and visit you, we are trying to get a free ticket for her, then she can come for 3-4 days.

How is Willie? How are things going with him going to the United States? Are you going to settle on the 1st of June?

Write soon, we are always glad to hear from you, best wishes from all of us. Hans

16 June 1950

Dear Mother,

I received your letter and the 20 DM. Thank you very much. The pictures of Father's grave and the little old room are nice. We are happy that everything is going well with you, please take care and do not overdo it. You are probably going to the cemetery every day and I am glad that you can do that. A lot of people here have buried their loved ones in their homeland with no one to care for them, but life goes on. Father had a long and good life.

Our request for a baby carriage was denied, so now I must figure out something else. Jamila would have liked to come for a visit. I could have gotten a free ticket with a doctor's approval (like Father's), but she cannot come without a baby carriage. The little one (Tom) is very well behaved, he stays the whole day outside on the grass in a children's bed. He has already gotten a nice tan and the children have lots of fun with him.

Lada (Don) will not be back until the end of August and Eva is traveling to Switzerland on the 2nd of July. I already got the pass and the Swiss Visa, paid 37 DM for them. Eva is going to get together with Lada.

Vlasta (Patricia) goes to school and stays with us. Vlasta and Honzik (John) go swimming with me and are nicely tanned. Jarmila is healthy, we have heard again from Milek (Jarmila's Brother). He did not write anything about Kralik's, I do not know what that means.

This week someone from here went back home, he was from Starkenbach, Switzerland. He had a wife and three children at home and could not get anywhere from here. I wonder if he will write.

We have received some nice clothing from the United States. Jarmila and I got 2 suits.

The weather is beautiful here, the sea water is warm, we can swim all day long. Eva and Vlasta (Patricia) learned to swim. Lada (Don) went on a school trip to the Alps and Eva was at Pfander and Bregenz, Austria.

I worry about the kids having a nice life and they find new things to learn, at home they would have had nothing.

How is Willie? I have a lot of clothes and things for children to sell, could he use some to sell? He could get a little money that way. He should write soon. What does he want to do?

We are going the end of September to the Australian Commission.

Please let me know when you all want to come. Was in Munich again on Wednesday, did not get to see Lene (Helene) since I had to go back in the afternoon.

Write soon and best wishes, Hans.

20 July 1950

Dear Mother,

I write to you from our new home in Tuttlingen, Germany. We started on Monday; everything was ready for us. We have two rooms; we are well taken care of. The camp is much larger than Czech, mostly Polish, Ukrainian, and Hungarian people are here. Also, from the Balten (Gypsies). Five minutes from camp is a swimming pool and around the whole city are mountains and forests. The town is as big as Trutnov and the Danube river flows through it. Not far from here is a spring. Main area is Stuttgart-Konstanz-Zurich. We like it here, but it is not as nice as it was at the Bodensee. We really liked the swimming.

We do not know how long we will be here; it does not seem to be too safe here. They are looking for volunteers from our group and the younger people are signing up. There is talk about sending us to Canada or the United States of America within 3 months. They need people to work, a new war is on the doorstep.

Eva writes nice letters and Lada (Don) has already turn into a Swiss person, has forgotten the Czech language and cannot write it anymore. Vlasta (Patricia) and Honzik (John) eat a lot.

Write soon to let us know when you can come and see us. How is Willie and his wife? Best wishes from all of us. Hans

J.H. Tuttlingen (Wuertt.) Post office Box

Envelope- Frau Berta Honolke, Neumarkt Obpf, Holzheim, postmark Feb. 20, 1950

26 December 1951

Dear Mother,

Since it was not possible for me to write before the holidays, I want to do this today. I am behind with everything, because of the relocation, and I must take care of everything myself because Jarmila cannot keep up with the language. And in such a big city there is a lot to do.

I received Willie's letter; I hope you received the coffee in time for the holidays. Also, Willie was right to keep the coat.

Now some about Christmas. 14 days before Christmas we got a lot of snow and it is cold. The cold continued over Christmas, so it really set the mood.

We had a nice Christmas, we got so many gifts from our friends that I cannot list everything. Eva has received a new radio, the children a lot of mechanical toys, a Christmas tree with electric lights, because they do not have candles here. Lots of new clothes, I got a new suit. We did not need anything this time because we got everything.

We were thinking of you a lot and wondered if you also had such a warm and beautiful home, but I believe that you do not have such a beautiful winter with that much of snow.

I will write Willie separately because I am waiting for a letter from a local organization. Hopefully Lene received her package before the holidays, if not it should be in Steinhöring by now.

Write me a detailed letter how you spent Christmas and when Lene left. Unfortunately, I have little time to write right now, because after work I learn English, which is the most important thing.

So, do not be angry with me I do not write often.

Warm greetings from all of us
Hans

Did you get the coffee in time for the holidays? I sent a 1/2 kg can in November.

Before I sent this letter, I received the letter from Lene with the 2 pictures, both of which are unbelievably beautiful. The beautiful winter weather continues, it was real Christmas weather. Christmas is a little different here than in Europe.

The big business advertisements come 4 weeks before Christmas. There are whole displays with large movable Christmas figures, one was a heavenly gate with Peter and Archangel standing in front of it, surrounded by angels which all moved, covered in artificial snow. That was something for Honzik and Vlasta. Toys in such a large selection and modern design as I have never seen them before.

The Christmas trees are set up 1 week before Christmas. There is no midnight mass, the first service is at 5 am. But they also sing Silent Night, although in English. We did not have to worry about anything. Two days before Christmas, at 10 o'clock in the evening, when the children were already asleep, some local people came and brought us a Christmas tree and set it up, also 24 electric candles, tree hangings and then they left again. We received gifts from our friends, so that each child had 7-8 gifts including mechanical toys. The two little guys had a lot of fun and we were up until am. Maxeras were with us too. Vlasta and Lada got roller skates, Eva a dress, Honzik a sleigh and Tomik got a bear that speaks.

From the Riebels, I got a panorama viewer with a lot of pictures from California, Florida, Colorado, and Tennessee.

From a friend, from Philadelphia, I got a new suit that fits me very well. Jarmila got a perfume from Coty-Paris. 1 coat, 1 pair of shoes and galoshes, 1 coffeemaker, and much more.

Since the children go to the St. Wenceslaus catholic school, they all received from the sisters rainboots (new), and the students from the high school donated us a big basket full of the finest different preserves, chocolate, bananas and much more. The basket weighed 50 pounds. They came by car, handed everything to Jarmila and wished us Merry Christmas. It may sound like a fairy tale to you but there are still a lot of good people here.

Eva was on the local radio in Cedar Rapids for a Christmas program. They broadcasted in a Czech Christmas program. We have 3 channels here; one broadcasts in Czech. Eva also sings in the St. Wenceslaus church choir. In Cedar Rapids there are 9 different churches, different creeds, 5 Catholic churches of which 2 of them are 2 Czech, Holy Ludmila and Holy Wenceslas. The sisters really like Honzik. Enough for today. Hans

14 September 1950

Dear Mom,

I received your wire and letter. I also received a wire of 15 DM from Hildegard today, but I do not know what for. The things I sent for Bärbel (Barbara) and Hildegard were free, I am not asking for anything. Can you ask what this is for?

As for your things I sent, you can money in November, if you can use the same. I just must divide everything so that I have some money every month. It is still enough for October. I already have a stroller; it is not as elegant as the one at home, but it is sufficient for today's conditions.

Lada (Don) and Eva came, they both look exceptionally good. Eva has gained 10 kg, Lada 4 kg.

Beginning September 10th, we must cook for ourselves, we received a kitchen stove, which is working well. For 10 days, we will receive a coupon to shop at local merchants. Vegetables for 10 days, 20 kg, 4 kg meat, 21 kg bread, 3kg. rolls, etc. butter 3kg. I must keep track of it to ensure that everything will be fine.

The Landowner to whom we are going to, from the United States, wrote us and sent a few photographs. He has 4 farms, 150 cattle, 6 horses, 3 tractors and modern machines. He is 78 years old and his children are away from home. He reserved a house for us.

Write again soon.

Greetings from everyone
Hans

Photo of the little one

23 November 1950

Dear Mom,

I would like to tell you more, since I sent my last postcard from Rastatt, Germany today. We were already called to the American doctor on Thursday, and they sent us to the visa department of the local consulate on the same day.

Friday morning at 11 a.m., we were introduced to the Consul of Bremen who granted us the entry permit.

We will be transported from Rastatt to Bremen, Germany on the 12th of March. We could have already left on the 5th of March, but we were granted a 1-week extension.

I will try to get the free ticket renewed and will try to come to Munich, Germany again.

Now our time is over, it has been over 2 years here in Germany, I liked it quite well. I will send more information later.

For the time being still sending greetings.
Hans

We go back to Diez on Tuesday.

16 December 1950

Dear Mom.

I want to write you in detail today to answer your last letter. Thursday, we were told to go immediately to Rastatt and Report to the American government. Friday morning, we drove through Koblenz, Mainz, Worms and Karlsruhe to Rastatt, Germany, where we temporarily live in the camp.

The camp is nice, within large and modern barracks. There is central heating everywhere and hot and cold running water. The food is good, and they have a particularly good children's menu.

We have already been documented, photographed, and fingerprinted. We hope that we will be finished with the whole procedure by Thursday-Friday and then could go back.

If all goes well, we can finally leave in April or/May, but that is also not certain, because just last week I was notified by the JRO that I could go to New Zealand.

I have agreed to it but will take whatever comes first, so that I can finally get away. New Zealand is 2,000 km from Australia, an island in the Pacific Ocean. It is the best emigration possibly; no winters and the climate are very mild. Eternal spring, I could bake oblates there. Only families are accepted. The island has 1 1/2 million residents, mostly English. Soon I will know more and will report more then.

27 May 1951

Dear Mom,

We received your letter today, as well as a letter from Willie with the enlarged photograph of the USNS Harry Taylor in Bremerhaven, Germany. The two small pictures in your letter are also quite good. By now, you should have also received the postcard from Chicago. We were in this skyscraper district. From there we continued to travel, Chicago – Milwaukee (at the Canadian border).

Tomik (Tomas) mastered the trip very well, as did Honzik (John) and Vlasta (Patricia). The food on the ship was particularly good.

In morning they had coffee, scrambled eggs, bread, semolina porridge or rice porridge and compote. Lunch: potatoes, meat, (plenty) salad, compote, 1 apple or 1 orange, tea. Dinner: potatoes, meat, vegetables, fruit, tea, bread you could take as much as you wanted.

There was a special menu for small children. There was no hunger. In New Orleans we were well looked after well by the American Red Cross. Soup, coffee, donuts, lemonade as much as you wanted. We ate a lot there, got tickets for over $50 and drove through the city in a beautiful limousine. Traveling by train is also pleasant because there are only padded seats in the United States with seats facing the direction of travel. There is cooled drinking water and every comfort in every car.

Our guarantor has 2 cars and a truck. There is no farmer here without a car, the nicest biggest cars. You do not see anyone walking by foot.

The food here is first class everywhere, soups are not cooked but for lunch and dinner meat, chickens, geese, compotes, pastries and always coffee.

Our farmer has 3 tractors, I drive the biggest one, which has 9 speeds. Corn is now being planted. Since school is already on break here, Lada (Don) is already schooled, and he drives with a small tractor. It is a lot of fun for him. We have it nice around our house now. We have a large garden as big as the garden in Trutnov. We have some forest, the fruit trees are now blooming, and lots of roses, the children could not have it any better. Tomik (Tom)can walk alone and will not need to be afraid that something will happen to him.

We also have a lot of wood to fire. Jarmila is a bit scared, but she will get used to it too. There are a lot of Czechs around us, even in the church service in in Czech. We have enough to eat here and we have received a lot from the people. Eva goes to school in Protivin, Iowa and she likes it too. She is being taught bay a nun, her parents came from Munich and Ingolstadt, Germany, she has relatives in Friedrichshafen. Eva speaks German to her.

About 30 km from here are German farmers, I want to go visit them next Sunday because of Willie.

Now I would like to ask, or tell Willie, to go to the customs office and ask whether he can send a chromatic harmonic here. In a package. They had nice ones in Limburg, Verdi or Traviata for 180 DM, I just did not have enough money there. He should say that I bought it in Germany and forgot to take it with me.

Maybe it can be declared as a gift. I would send you the money in $ (dollars). Then inquire about Jenisch shoes, there are supposed to be nice ones in Germany. On Sunday, I will inquire at the post office about sending a package to Germany. I could possibly also send something.

Willie and Lene should not be angry that I have not written yet, I have little time right now. Plus, the large garden, I planted everything, potatoes, peas, corn, herbs, cucumbers, lettuce etc.

For the time being you do not have to worry, you must work everywhere, we live unbelievably beautiful and healthy.

Write to me soon regarding the harmonica.

Greetings from everyone
Hans

Did you receive the package from the United States?

17 August 1951

Dear Mom,

I received your letter and the package. I am enjoying the nice shoes, the Nivea just ran out, it came at the right time.

They do not produce good shoes here; everything is worn until it is worn out and then you just buy new things. Same thing with clothes, dressmakers and tailors have no businesses here. I also received Willie's letter with the message that the package is on its way. I am putting together your package; I will also add coffee and peanut butter. I will send Lene's to Steinhoering. Tell us how the current situation is, there is a lot of military personnel from here going to Germany.

Last week we received new furniture for our second living room. It is an extendable divan (dark blue) that can be used as a bed at night, a table with two leather armchairs and showcase. Now we have everything furnished. 3 bedrooms, 2 living rooms, kitchen, and a small back room.

The furniture was donated by a rich family from Cedar Rapids. We live better today than ever before, and we live more comfortably and better than in Europe. Especially regarding food, we have everything, last week I bought a bushel (that is 34 kg) of peaches in Cedar Rapids for $3. They came from California in such large quantities that the merchants were happy to sell them. We get meat and baked goods for free, especially sausages - every day, the children eat a lot, and everyone looks good. We get bread baked from the baker Maxera (who studied in Trutnov), cakes and pies for free for the whole week.

Eva is always in Cedar Rapids and has already saved a few dollars. Sunday, we went on a half-day car ride through the forests of the Iowa River, drove through the German town of Amana, Iowa a German settlement from 1890 to 1900.

What about Willie, is he back at work through the workforce center for a few months or is he still unemployed?

As for my work, you do not have to worry, have enough variety in the workshop, making sausages, in the smokehouse, driving to pick up cattle or delivering goods with the delivery vehicles, a lot of ice is ground because everything must be cooled. We work from 7 a.m. – 12 a.m. and 1 p.m. – 4 p.m., after work I take a shower, change my clothes and at 4:30 p.m. I am off work.

This month, it has already been 2 years since Lene was with us in Lindau, Germany.

I love to think back to the beautiful Lake Constance. If you have time, write again soon.

Greetings from everyone
Hans

8 October 1951

Dear Mother,

Thank you for your letter from 3 October 1951 and the one from before with the articles from the Nurnberger Newspaper. In our newspaper here were pictures also from the train from Prague. The American organization paid the leader of the train $100 Dollars to bring the train to Selb, Germany (Konvalinka) an also made him an honor citizen. About 20 people from the train will travel to Canada, Bata in Canada helped them.

On Oct 28th we will have a great celebration to honor the ASR. The Governor of Iowa declared that day as a holiday for all Czech people. Everything has an anticommunist flavor.

We went on Saturday evening 14 days ago to a concert in Swisher where a Mahrishe Band from Chicago played. (Sekacova maravska kapela Chicago) Lots of Czech music, polkas and Waltzes, there was singing also. We danced until 3 am. Jarmila had enough then. It was lots of fun.

I bought a stove and 2 tons of coal this week. It has been cold already, so we must heat the house, the stove does that. We have decorated everything nicely; you would like it. Everything is nice in the whole house and warm.

The children are going to an English school in Walford, Iowa. Eva does extremely well in school, she speaks English good already. Eva goes with me to Cedar Rapids every Saturday. She works in a bakery where she puts the bread into a machine to slice. She gets paid 5 dollars and 2 big sacks of cookies. She already paid for her own shoes and underwear. Here in the United States of America the parents do not give anything to them when they marry, they are on their own. You do not have to worry about my work, I am used to it, the main thing is that it pays well, I make a good living. Twice a week we have pork schnitzel, also Goulash, Paprika, chicken etc. No one eats hot dogs anymore, everyone had enough of them.

Jarmila's clothes do not fit anymore, everything is too small. Lada runs around on a bicycle, Vlasta and Honzik have a lot of English friends and the little Tomik (Tom) is happy and handsome. I am happy with everything; we never had a nice home like we have now.

I sent Willie 2 packages with clothes, for Hildegard a nice winter coat, also one for Willie, but his is not as nice and he might have to fix it up. Also sent him a pair of black shoes. A can of coffee and peanut butter was also in the package and some nice dresses for Hildegard. Eva thanks you for the Harmonica, that was her wish. I am going to send you some coffee and other things for it. Hope you received the package with the coat, shoes, etc.

Let me know if the coat fits, if not you can sell it. If you have a wish for anything let me know. I am looking for a coat for Lene, hope to find one soon. Willie sent me a picture of his family, I gave it to some German American that lives here, they are looking for a sponsor for him. It takes a little time and patience. Was 2 years in the camps before I got the chance to come here.

Kralik is not doing well in Trutnov, Czech Republic. Old Kralik forgot his age and there is no business anymore. He is 70 years old and has nothing. Maria must take care of the old people. We can send things from here, but they must pay a lot of taxes on the packages, the communist does not like that.

If you have a picture of father's grave could you send one. We think and talk a lot about father, it is too bad that he could not see things as there are now, he would have like that.

> Write when you can and all the best from us,
> Hans.

26 December 1951

Dear Mother,

Since it was not possible for me to write before the holidays, I want to do this today. I am behind with everything, because of the relocation, and I must take care of everything myself because Jarmila cannot keep up with the language. And in such a big city there is a lot to do.

I received Willie's letter; I hope you received the coffee in time for the holidays. Also, Willie was right to keep the coat.

Now some about Christmas. 14 days before Christmas we got a lot of snow and it is cold. The cold continued over Christmas, so it really set the mood.

We had a nice Christmas, we got so many gifts from our friends that I cannot list everything. Eva has received a new radio, the children a lot of mechanical toys, a Christmas tree with electric lights, because they do not have candles here. Lots of new clothes, I got a new suit. We did not need anything this time because we got everything.

We were thinking of you a lot and wondered if you also had such a warm and beautiful home, but I believe that you do not have such a beautiful winter with that much of snow.

I will write Willie separately because I am waiting for a letter from a local organization. Hopefully Lene received her package before the holidays, if not it should be in Steinhöring by now.

Write me a detailed letter how you spent Christmas and when Lene left. Unfortunately, I have little time to write right now, because after work I learn English, which is the most important thing.

So, do not be angry with me I do not write often.

Warm greetings from all of us
Hans

Did you get the coffee in time for the holidays? I sent a 1/2 kg can in November.

Before I sent of the letter, I received the letter from Lene with the 2 pictures, both of which are unbelievably beautiful. The beautiful winter weather continues, it was real Christmas weather. Christmas is a little different here than in Europe.

The big business advertisements come 4 weeks before Christmas. There are whole displays with large movable Christmas figures, one was a heavenly gate with Peter and Archangel standing in front of it, surrounded by angels which all moved, covered in artificial snow. That was something for Honzik and Vlasta. Toys in such a large selection and modern design as I have never seen them before.

The Christmas trees are set up 1 week before Christmas. There is no midnight mass, the first service is at 5 am. But they also sing Silent Night, although in English. We did not have to worry about anything. Two days before Christmas, at 10 o'clock in the evening, when the children were already asleep, some local people came and brought us a Christmas tree and set it up, also 24 electric candles, tree hangings and then they left again. We received gifts from our friends, so that each child had 7-8 gifts including mechanical toys. The two little guys had a lot of fun and we were up until 1am. Maxeras were with us too. Vlasta and Lada got roller skates, Eva a dress, Honzik a sleigh and Tomik got a bear that speaks.

From the Riebels, I got a panorama viewer with a lot of pictures from California, Florida, Colorado, and Tennessee.

From a friend, from Philadelphia, I got a new suit that fits me very well. Jarmila got a perfume from Coty-Paris. 1 coat, 1 pair of shoes and galoshes, 1 coffeemaker, and much more.

Since the children go to the St. Wenceslaus catholic school, they all received from the sisters rainboots (new), and the students from the high school donated us a big basket full of the finest different preserves, chocolate, bananas and much more. The basket weighed 50 pounds. They came by car, handed everything to Jarmila and wished us Merry Christmas. It may sound like a fairy tale to you but there are still a lot of good people here.

Eva was on the local radio in Cedar Rapids for a Christmas program. They broadcasted in a Czech Christmas program. We have 3 channels here; one broadcasts in Czech. Eva also sings in the St. Wenceslaus church choir. In Cedar Rapids there are 9 different churches, different creeds, 5 Catholic churches of which 2 of them are 2 Czech, Holy Ludmila and Holy Wenceslas

The sisters really like Honzik. Enough for today, Hans

28 December 1951

Our Good Dear Ommi,

To beginning with, I ask you not to be angry that you had to wait so long for a message from me. If I write as many letters as I have thoughts of all of you, then you should be satisfied. There is not a day when I do not think of all my loved ones. I am also very often afraid and would be happy if you could all visit us, then I could say that I am satisfied. But above all, what is dear to me is so far from here. Our American friends are all nice to us, take care of us, are very respectable, despite everything I cannot forget my home and will never forget. May God grant that I can come back there and find all of you in good health.

Dear Ommi,

The mail has just arrived with a letter from Helene, I am happy about every message from you. The pictures are very pretty.

The tomb at the father's grave turned out exceptionally good, I really like it. But it would be better if the good one was among us again. It is hard to understand that he is gone forever. I feel the emptiness and know how hard it is for you. A lot has lost its value, Ledo was a great support for you. I often think how nice it would be, if a message would come from him and tell us what he thinks of everything. It is a pity that everything happened the way it did and that dear Ledo can no longer experience all the joys with you. He would have deserved it. My father and Ledo were the best.

I had to drive so far for me to know the value of my love for you all. They say: "Only when you lose something, do you know what you have lost", that is so true. The picture of you with Bärble (Barbara) is also quite nice. Bärble is a little beauty. Ledo was so good joking around with the children. Bärble looks nice in the coat from Vlasta (Patricia), I am happy that she can wear it. And the plush coat fits you perfectly. It is good that you have it, you will need a warm coat for this cold season in your area. I was happy when I got the coat myself and thought of you, how well it will fit you. I can see, from the picture, that you finally got a water pump. Hans and I often talked about how dangerous it is for you. We did not like it at all. Now it is okay.

31 December 1951

Dear Ommi,

I would like to walk and come visit you. I always liked it very much to be with you. Hans and I often talk about you and your cozy room.

Dear Ommi,

Write us and tell us how you spent Christmas. I want to paint a picture of ours for you. I did not look forward to Christmas at all. I had quite large expenses due to our emigration.

Therefore, we had little money left for Christmas. But everything turned out differently. The first gift came on Friday before Christmas Eve.

The children go to school at St. Wenceslaus church, are being taught by nuns. And they organized everything, I am going to tell you. So, the students from high school (that is like our public school) brought large basket full of different preserves, apples, cookies, sweets etc. and gifts for children. Eva got a nice sweater, Lada (Don) a game, Vlasta (Patricia) a doll, Honzik (John) a coloring books with paint to color. From the nuns, Hans received a statue of St. Josef, I got handmade blankets (small). Eva got shoes and a sweater, pullover, Lada got galoshes and paint to color, Vlasta got a beautiful doll and a summer dress. Honzik got red pants and red sweater, Tomik got a game.

The same day we got a basket of food from the monastery in Cedar Rapids, Iowa. I wish you could have seen how beautiful everything was wrapped and tied.

From the Riebels we got valuable things. Hans received a panoramic viewer with pictures from America. It is a brand-new thing. The pictures are plastic, and they look so natural. There are also pictures of Indians. Eva received a nylon set - brush, mirror, and comb, I have not seen anything more beautiful. Another dress, sweater, a fountain pen, and pencils with the engraved name 'Eva'.

Lada got roller skates, and a fountain pen with pencil engraved with 'Vladimir' (Don). Vlasta receive a white fur stole with collar. Honzik got a game, horses with carriage and coachman, you can harness the horse. Tomik received a wooden workbench with hammer and screws, where he can screw and hammer, which he loves to do. He also got a teddy. Whenever you wind him up, he plays like an old picture (??? *possibly dances or plays music*). And I got a beautiful Gobelin (tapestry) wallet and nylon petticoat with fine lace, also a set of fine perfume and lipstick.

The Riebel family are fine and quite rich people, just like the gifts. From the baker Maxera in Cedar Rapids, Eva was gifted a set of cases for stockings, linen and handkerchiefs all lined with plastic, also a white dress with bolero, red pearls, and earrings for the summer. Lada got ice skates and a nice wallet. Vlasta Rollschue, Honzik a large tank, Tomik a rubber car, tractor, and a tank.

Friends from New Orleans and Durheim and Cedar Rapids also sent nice gifts. Eva got a coat, sweater, socks, silk scarfs, handkerchiefs, perfume, bracelet, and earrings, from the Riebel's she also got galoshes, Lada got socks, several games, and a toy car, from Hans he got a nice winter jacket, hat, pants, shirt, and from the Riebel's shoes. Vlasta got socks and games and nylon apron and a red hat (cap). Honzik received lots of toys and socks and so did Tomik.

I got coffee maker, powder and perfume set, and a candy dish from Hans. From the children I got a glasses, knife, and large fork set, and Kaffetüpfel (*coffee? possibly biscuits or coffee flavor*). I am thankful. I got Hans slippers and a fountain pen. Hans got a gray suit from friends of the Riebel's, it fits him fabulous and is worth $60. Two Czech men visited us, who are also refugees. They brought Hans an electrical shaving device, a nice new radio and perfume for Eva and for Lada and Honzik cowboy hats. Vlasta and Tomik also got little things. We also got a basket with California apples from the Kralik family who are distant relatives on my father's side.

The children got a lot of sweets, oranges, nuts, etc. We also got some particularly good stollen (*yeas pastry*) from Maxera. Hans's coworker and his wife brought a small Christmas tree and decorated it.

All our friends only had the wish to make our first Christmas in America nice and special. We were so happy about everything we have received and are incredibly grateful for these good people. We did not expect that. We also received $18. People in America are very generous. America is an extraordinarily rich country.

Now I want to tell you about our little house. We have a very warm home; we can heat all day and night. In the kitchen there is a water heater boiler for hot water, so we always have hot water in the bathroom and kitchen. All together we have 6 rooms including the kitchen, plus a bathroom and open and an enclosed patio.

The attic is also spacious and warm, so we can store different things up there. There are no wardrobes closets for clothes in America. Every house has built-in closets. This is a very practical thing, saving a lot of space in the homes. I bought new plastic curtains for our windows. Our home may not be as elegant as our home at home, but it is quite friendly and cozy and practical.

Eva and Vlasta have a bedroom, Lada and Honzik have one and Tomik sleeps together with us. I got a crib for Tomik, there, the good dear boy finally has a decent resting place.

Tomik is such a good and well-behaved boy. Hans is incredibly happy with him; we all love him very much. Teta Helenka likes to see Honzik. He is very personable and is the most popular child in school. The sisters say: "I don't know what it is about the child, but everyone who sees him must love him". At home we have a lot of fun with him, he speaks unique dialects. Eva speaks English well and was even on the radio in Cedar Rapids, Iowa for a Christmas program.

Lada and Vlasta help me a lot around the house. I always have a lot to do. We have a lot of visitors.

I am lying in bed with the flu for the second time this winter. The weather here is very harsh, and I am no longer as tough as I used to be. The children are on Christmas break and that is why I can afford to lie in bed. Mail came with your letter. You look so good in the photograph; you look so young. You home is nice. I wanted to make you happy for Christmas and wanted to buy you the same curtains that I have in my kitchen. But I could not make it happen due to little time and money. But when I go to town, I will get them and send it to you. Then you can write me how you like them. The gravestone at father's grave is beautiful, the poor man has at least an illusion of home from his grave, since he cannot rest in his home country. In the summer, the alp flowers will bloom at his grave and the idyllic giant mountain scene will be complete.

I will stop writing for today. I still have a lot to write but Hans has a lot to do by correcting my mistakes. He has little time and patience.

Please give our regards to Lene und Hildegard, kiss little Bärble for me and Willie, too. And you are warmly embraced and greeted by us all.

Yours, Jarmila

I am happy that Hildegard is satisfied with the things I sent. Now, I will look for something for Lene. Plush coats are not available as they are not in fashion. Got some here but everything is too small. Greetings to Mrs. Horing. Jarmila

14 December 1952

Dear Mother,

We hope that the package has arrived, and you have a few nice things for Christmas. Should the black fur jacket not fit, sell it?

We got your last letter, also thank you for the knitted things, they have not arrived yet but should get here before Christmas.

I sent Lene (Helene) a package also with a beautiful coat, do not know if it will fit. If she does not like the color, she can have it dyed.

We will celebrate Christmas like always, the celebrations in the United States are not as nice as in Europe.

I am also sending Willie a package and a letter.

Write soon and stay healthy.

Hans

Envelope: Frau Berta Honolke, Holzheim, Neumarkt/Obpf., Germany

John Honolka, 1507 Hamilton St. SW, Cedar Rapids-Iowa USA

5 January 1954

Dear Mother.

I wish you the best for the New Year, especially health and contentment. The package arrived exactly on the 24th of Dec, enough time to put it under the Christmas tree. The best is the Nivea cream, our family is used to it. The filled wafer pieces were especially good but not necessary, you should not have spent so much money.

Hope you got my package on time and there were no problems because of the 3 cans of coffee. I was waiting for Lene (Helene) to write. We have sales now and with the lowered prices I could buy some things she might need; it is hard to figure out from here what she might like or need.

It is not easy to write, do not have a lot of time, so much to do. After work I have things to do that a wife would normally do. She (Jarmila) does not even go to the store, even so the stores are only 5 minutes away and in all the stores they speak Czech, the same thing at home.

It was cold on Christmas but no snow. It is not the same as it was at home, 8 days before Christmas the tree is put up and then taken down right after the holidays. I bought an electric train set for little Tommy and Honzik (John). For all the others I bought boots and clothes they needed. I got some pajamas and warm slippers. A young Czech was visiting over Christmas, he was in camp with us in Germany. He is from Melnik, Czechoslovakia, he came to the United States of America with his father. His father died on the 1st of November and he had nowhere to go for Christmas. He is in the Air Force and had leave over the holidays. He went to school in Litomerice, Czechoslovakia. He brought presents for the children and a radio for Lada (Don). Lada and Eva took him skiing.

The children go ice skating all the time. They like it here and they speak English fluently and I think it would be hard for them to go back to Europe.

We are free here and we can do what we want. When it comes to Willie, I can only recommend that he thinks about coming here when things in Neumarkt get settled. It is for young people, if I told you all the details about my life here the first few years he might not like the idea. Eva and Lada make some money and Jarmila cleans the radio station KPLS in Cedar Rapids, about 20 minutes away from us. Everybody helps, and we are moving forward. With me it was a need, I could not stay in Germany.

Hope he liked the package I send; he probably needed the things. We received mail from Trutnov, Kralik works for the military, he repairs boots. Zdenek is in the military and Misses Kralik gets a pension. They are extremely poor. Maria works in Farschnitz, Austria in a new factory.

If things go right this summer, we will move either to California or Oregon, looking for the warm weather. There they have a big Rose parade around Christmas, it is green there always and you can grow roses and walk beneath the palm trees. The weather here is not so nice, 6 months hot and 6 months cold. No spring or fall. Already feel the arthritis.

Write soon, best wishes from all of us.

Hans

30 July 1957

Dear Mother,

I receive your last letter as well as Corllis letters, I am sending you the completed form for the consulate. It took a little longer because I still do not know on which date the trip can happen. Your ticket is booked through the travel agency. It was ordered in Chicago, but I am still waiting on a date, when there is a free space on the airplane for you, there are all booked in advance for a long time. I wanted that arrive in Chicago on September 14, because I am off on Saturday and Sunday.

Lene, can come visit in a couple of years, she is still young. The airline Pan America have German speaking crews.

As soon as I hear from Chicago, I will let you know. Be sure your papers and visa are in order and are valid for 6 months.

Willie should write to the consulate right away. Greetings, Hans

On page 2 of the Sundays Post (newspaper), you will find an article about the massacre in Aussig.

16 August 1957

Dear Mother,

Today, I received the news that your airline ticket has been issued for Pan America under your name, Mrs. Honolke. Departure from Frankfurt, September 13, and arrival September 14 in Chicago, where we will meet you.

Hopefully, you got your visa and papers in order since there is only 4 weeks left. There is no time left.

I am sending you another newspaper with another article on page 2. I am spreading the news and will write right away.

Greetings

Hans

10 April 1958

Dear Mother,

We have now arrived safely in California; the road trip was unbelievably bad. We got into a sandstorm in the desert in New Mexico, then in the state of Arizona, we had to cross mountains in snowstorms, so we were on the road for 6 days, we have traveled 3000 kilometers. We found a nice house in Pasadena, a suburb of Los Angeles.

There are palms, lemon, orange and olive trees around the house, and everything is green all winter long, there is snow on the mountains, it is nice here.

The two little boys are already in school, Lada (Don) and Vlasta (Patricia) are finishing school in Amana, then they will follow by train.

So far everything is going well, I am sending you some pictures of California. I have about 20 minutes to work by car, it is a large company, 5 times the size of Amana.

We drive an hour to the Pacific Ocean. Hollywood is here too. The number of unemployed has risen to 5 1/2 million and there is little hope of better times. So, Willie should be happy.

I will write again soon. Greetings, Hans

1016 N Summit Ave
Pasadena – Calif. USA

16 December 1958

Dear Mother,

Please forgive me that I have not written in so long. Since July, I am back in Cedar Rapids, where we used to live. I am working in a large pastry bakery and for the last 2 months I have been the manager of one of the bakeries that the company owns. They own 4 bakeries.

The Amana Germans visited 14 days ago and recruited me for their large bakery in South Amana where we were until March, so after Christmas I am back in my old position.

Their bakery lost over $15,000 in profit under the new management, so they want me to bring the bakery back up again.

I am back from California because neither Lada (Don) or Vlasta (Patricia) wanted to come to us and Jarmila cannot be alone. She suffers from melancholy, hallucinations and has attempted suicide three times. We try everything possible, unfortunately my financial resources are exhausted so there is nothing else we can do but to take care of her.

Vlasta got married in September, she has a nice apartment in South Amana. Her husband is from a farm, they are wealthy and decent people of German origin, their name is Grimm.

After Christmas she will help me in the bakery. Lada has the prospect of a college scholarship and will become an athletics coach.

Honzik und Tommy are both grown up, both are a real joy. Eva is with her husband, he is already a Lieutenant, in Boston, she is very well looked after.

Otherwise, I do not know anything about Trautenau or anywhere else.

I am sending you $15, ten dollars are meant for you as a Christmas present and for $5 send me 2 boxes of Nivea, by airmail, to my new address in South Amana, Iowa.

As soon as I hear from you, I will write back immediately. Spend Christmas as usual and do not worry.

Your son, Hans

.

JULY 8, 2019 EVA HONOLKA NEWMAN SILENCED

DURING 1989 I MET THE entire Honolka clan. PC Callahan and Arvis Williams had been by Eva's side for many years. At first, I thought they were "Honolka's". Over the past 34 years I have heard Eva share her life and feelings from her heart numerous times. Always ending by saying privately "we have to finish my book". It is not known how many years PC and Arvis started typing her almost illegible handwriting.

In May of 2019, Don and I went to visit her in Bessemer, AL for her 82nd birthday. Once again listening to segments of her life. I asked, "where are these writings"? Slowly rising from her new couch, in her new apartment, in her new city, she retrieved a small well-worn leather attaché case. With tears in her eyes as she handed it to me she said, "this is all that I can find". I was given permission to take the attaché case back to Texas to be copied and returned. Somehow, I had made the promise to tell her story. You are almost done reading her story.

Back in Texas, as I stood at my copier, I was being incredibly careful not to disturb the order of the documents. At that time, I did not know there was no order. Every page was photocopied and placed back into her attaché case; in the order I received the papers. The following morning a special trip was made to the post office to return her documents in her attaché case as promised, priority mail.

During the next three weeks Eva and I had several lengthy conversations. Helping me a great deal with dates and time frames. I loved listening to her soft tender voice through her Czech accent. She was so excited that her story was finally going to be documented.

A few pages were sent priority mail on Monday the 3rd of June, 2019. I felt it was important to let her know I was working on her book.

Her call to me on Thursday, June 13th was bittersweet. Her voice sounded sad and tired. She said, "it had been an emotional weekend in Atlanta, GA." The highlight of returning to her apartment was opening my envelope and reading a few pages of her journey.

As we began to talk about her book, you could hear her tone change. She became like a different person. Her enthusiasm came over the telephone. She was excited. Sharing I would not be available to work of her story for over a month and we agreed we would resume our conversations mid-July.

At 1:30 p.m. on Monday, July 8, 2019 one of Eva's neighbors called me because she could not get hold of Mike or Julie. She had not seen Eva since Saturday night, so she went into her apartment and found her in bed, fully cloth with what she was wearing Saturday, July 6th. She was staring at the ceiling of her small bedroom with Whiskey, her cat, resting on her hair. She called 911. Keeping me on the telephone answering questions for paramedics. Fortunately, via text, I was able to contact Julie and she met the ambulance at the hospital.

The medical community diagnosed a moderate stroke leaving her paralyzed on her right side and silenced. Eva's greatest strength of communicating with others, suddenly gone forever.

For some unknown reason, Don and I made a quick decision to take a road trip to Ozark, Montgomery and Bessemer, Alabama leaving Texas on February 29, 2020. We had not seen John, Jarmila, Chip and the Walker boys' headstones. We traveled to the home where "The Newman's" resided in 1969. Continued to Montgomery to visit PC's widow, Nesta, and then on to Bessemer to see Eva for a few days. Not knowing it would be our last visit.

The following week on March 8, 2020 Arben Skivjani and his lovely family visited. You could see the love in Eva's face in videos and pictures. Arben was like another son. Eva had enjoyed Mother's Day and her Birthday with Arben in 2019, just two months prior to her stroke.

Patrik and Rachel Ricica also visited many times, sharing pictures with us.

On March 13, 2020 President Donald J. Trump would declare COVID-19 a National Emergency. Within a week Nursing Homes across the country were in lockdown. Banning family from visiting loved ones.

Prior to Eva's stroke she often shared with her siblings Don, John, Patricia, and Tom. feelings of loneliness. The highlight of the day took placed in the early morning hours when Mike would call on his way home from work. Often sitting in his driveway not to wake sleeping family members. It was also comforting for Eva to know Julie was less than 5 minutes away.

Some may say Eva was collateral damage of Covid-19 seclusion. That is their opinion. It is my opinion she died just like her Mother, Jarmila. She died of a broken heart.

Her death certificate said natural causes. Hemiplegia and Hemiparesis following Cerebral Infraction affecting right dominant side. It is my own personal belief that she willed herself to death. She knew what awaited her, she had a strong faith, she lost one of her many gifts and talents – her voice. For a year and one half she laid or sat planning her next step. Eva had the final word at the end –she willed her homecoming.

As each of us walk this earth, we are unique in our own way. Eva was one of a kind, not duplicable. Hopeful you have gained a sense of her passion, purpose, and personality. The world is better because John Honolka, Sr. brought his family to the United States of America. Those that had a privileged, and a true privilege it was, to personally know his eldest, Eva Honolka Newman.

I sincerely hope you have enjoyed reading about the remarkable Honolka family and their courage through the eyes and words of Eva Honolka Newman.

TIME GOES ON

2020 Julie Remembers her Mom, Eva
May 14, 1937 – September 12, 2020

FAMILY AND FRIENDS THANK YOU for coming here today to remember my mom. My name is Julie and Eva was my mom.

My mom was a unique human who was more than any of us can fully comprehend. She endured many challenges that gave her an undeniable strength that endured throughout her life.

She guided me and my brother through life with compassion, wisdom, and generosity because these things were what encapsulated who she was.

My mother taught me many things but the one that meant the most was the importance of family.

The first memories I have of my mom are from Columbus, Georgia. We moved there in 1963 from Germany. She loved to be outside with us and she constantly looked for things to do with us that involved being outside. She would often make a picnic lunch for us and we would go to the backyard and eat lunch on a blanket. It was like an adventure for us. She would take us swimming a lot and take us on long walks to the lake.

She made Christmas special for us. She was an excellent at cooking and decorating. Christmas eve was always one of my favorite meals goose with potato dumplings. I remember we had an 8-foot aluminum tree that she decorated with beautiful glass ornaments. It even had one of those revolving color wheels. I loved that tree and thought it was the most beautiful tree ever. She always took the time to wrap our presents so perfectly. We even got to open one each Christmas eve.

I remember when we lived in Oklahoma when we were 8,6, and 4. My mom would give us 25 dents each and we would walk about 8 blocks to the five and dime store and buy a sack of candy and little toys, she taught us to be independent and she trusted us.

One of my favorite memories is when we lived in Ozark, Alabama Eva's mom and dad moved to Ozark for a short time and they happened to live in Ozark when Ozark got a record 8 inches of snow and my grandfather thought it was funny how crazy people were going over this snow. Ozark rarely got snow.

My mom instilled in us the love for bowling. She had us kids join a youth bowling league at Fort Rucker. Every Saturday she would drop us off to bowl and would give us $1.00 for lunch. I loved it because I always got a chili dog, french fries and a coke. I also remember when we lived in Columbus, Georgia, my mom, and dad were in a bowling league and we would go to a playroom while they bowled.

Eva loved yard work when we lived in Ozark our yard always looked good. We would often get the neighborhood yard of the month award. I used to think she was crazy because she would use the hose to wash the gutters in the street surrounding our yard, everything had to look perfect. She loved her banana trees and elephant ears and passed that love down to me.

Eva was an excellent baker. She made cakes for cake walks at school and PTA events, sometimes she made cakes shaped like school buses. She also made weddings cakes and many cakes to celebrate special occasions at The First White House of the Confederacy where she worked for many years.

And we must mention sauerbraten and dumplings. It is my most favorite meal in the world. Many times when I would visit her in Montgomery. Alabama she would make it for me.

Eva loved cats and because of that Mike and I are cat people. We got our first cat in 1968 a Siamese named Sam. She had several; cats after Sam but her most special cat was named Whiskey. Whiskey was more like a dog. When Eva moved to Birmingham, Alabama in March of 2018, Whiskey came with her. He would follow Eva to the dining room where she had lunched every day and would visit with everyone there. Sometimes Eva would let him stay with other people in their apartments. Everyone there loved whiskey.

Eva's life had many obstacles yet her perseverance through adversity is a powerful lesson for us and I believe is her legacy. What a wonderful lesson she gave us. Do not let adversities or setbacks or any distractions of the world keep you from what is most important in life.

How many people in this world have it so much easier than our Mom did? But through everything she went through she managed to keep her faith through all her trials. That is a wonderful legacy.

2020 Obituary of Eva Honolka Newman

Mrs. Eva Honolka Newman, age 83, passed away on September 13, 2020. The family will have a celebration of life for Mrs. Newman on Monday, October 12, 2020, with visitation at 10:30 A.M. and service at 11:00 A.M. at Frazer United Methodist Church in Montgomery, Alabama. Followed by interment in the Westview Memorial Cemetery in Ozark, Alabama, Holman Funeral Home and Cremations of Ozark is entrusted with local arrangements.

Eva was born May 14, 1937, in Trutnov, Czechoslovakia. The eldest daughter of the late John and Jarmila Honolka. For thirty-three years she was employed by the State of Alabama as a receptionist and tour guide at the state capitol and the First White House of the Confederacy. She always held in her heart her love for her homeland and for her adopted home country. Eva is now free to share how great this country is and the freedoms that it provided for her and her family.

In addition to her parents, she is preceded in death by her husband, LTC Frank Charles Newman and sons, Michael Frank Newman, Steven Allen Newman, John Zeke Walker and Sidney Honolka Walker.

She is survived by her two children, son, Michael Newman (Susan); daughter, Julie Slaten (Gary). She leaves behind her sister, Pat Shaver and her brothers, John Honolka (Sandy), Don Honolka (Sharon) and Tom Honolka (Leslie). She also leaves behind five grandchildren, Melanie Newman, Kelly Slaten, Stephanie (Newman) Burris, Brian Slaten, Amy Slaten and one great granddaughter Selah Burris.

2020 Eulogy for Eva Honolka Newman

May 14, 1937 – September 12, 2020
Given by her youngest brother, Tomas Honolka

October 12, 2020
Frazer United Methodist Church
6000 Atlanta Hwy
Montgomery. AL 76012

Proverbs 31: 29-31 NIV

"Many women do noble things, but you surpass them all. Charm is deceptive, and beauty is fleeting; but a woman who fears the lord is to be praised. Give her the reward she has earned, and let her works bring her praise at the city gate".

Today we come to praise Eva Honolka Newman who loved her God, her family, and her countries. Countries in the plural for Eva Honolka was an American citizen and patriot born in 1937 in Trutnov, Czechoslovakia to John Honolka and Jarmila Kralik. She was the first born and eldest of (5) children. Eva, Vladimir (Don), Vlasta (Patricia), John and myself Tomas.

I have been asked to say a few words about my sister Eva. It will be an impossible task to share Eva's journey through her life. Her trials, tribulations, tears, laughter, and accomplishments.

I want to thank all of you for your attendance here today. I want to thank Frazer United Methodist church and the staff. I acknowledge our most honored guest today, that being our lord and savior Jesus Christ. I extend condolences to Eva's immediate family for the loss of your mother, mentor, sister and to all in attendance for the loss of this beautiful spirit and soul.

Upon learning of Eva Honolka's passing my son Benjamin told me "Eva was a very impressive woman" and Eva was.

Who was Eva? What was Eva? Why was Eva the way she was? What influenced Eva's life? How was Eva molded and shaped? To understand Eva Honolka, one needs to understand her journey.

Eva Honolka was born shortly before the world exploded in 1939 into a world war that lasted 6 bloody years until 1945. It involved 100 million people from 30 countries. It was the deadliest conflict in human history with 70 to 85 million fatalities. Prior to this explosion Germany claimed rights to the Sudetenland, an area with a predominately ethnic German population and Czechoslovakia. These were the homes of John Honolka and Jarmila Kralik. This war was the beginning of an epic journey for Eva and the Honolka family on this earth.

An incident of that war that Eva's brother Don remembers is one example of The Honolka families experience of world war two. The family then lived in the city of Nova Paka; my brother Don remembers the German troops monthly searches of our house. The intimidation of dogs and fully armed troops pounding on your door at any hour of the day or night. Lining you up against the wall at gun point while searching and if anything was found you that you should not have you were shot. Don tells me this terrified everyone including Eva. Such experiences change a person forever. It changed the Honolka family. This was part of Eva's journey. It changed Eva. The courage to face fear and to overcome adversity had begun.

At the close of the war in 1945 John Honolka established his own business called "Koruna Fancy pastries". In less than 3 years the business was booming. John had become what he had always wanted to be, a man with an idea that had found its time and was now a tangible working reality that provided jobs for his assistants, delectable treats for his customers and the good things of life for his family. Johns fundamental traits of willingness to take a risk, personal initiative, self-reliance, and hard work had paid off.

However, suddenly, and overnight, a different world emerged. Friends became distrustful of friends, brothers turned against brothers, neighbors against neighbors as the Czech government was taken over by communists. John had become a capitalist in a communist land. He became an enemy of the state.

As children are wont to do at times, they will become children. In a spate of name calling, and this is what little Eva did, during an exchange with a neighbor child one day little Eva resorted to the most demeaning title her little thought process could conjure up, "You, you, communist you".

Within hours John Honolka was taken into custody for interrogation and jailed for indoctrinating his children against communism and its benefits. Johns business was nationalized, was told that "no man should own so much, or control this many worker's, this is only permitted to the state. John Honolka became an enemy of the state.

For brevity's sake the Honolka family escaped, John was caught, prisoned, and beaten. The family was split up for 9 months and with the aid of the American red cross was reunited with his family in the French sector of Austria, the city of Salzburg to be exact.

The ordeal and accompanying deprivations continued as the Honolka family waited out three long years in the displaced persons camps agonizingly slow process of immigrating to America. Such experiences change a person forever. It changed the Honolka family. It changed Eva. Eva Honolkas resilience, courage, strong will and pride for her family develops. Now a new chapter opens:

Deuteronomy 8:7-10 NIV

"for the Lord, your GOD is bringing you into a good land, a land with streams and pools of water with springs flowing in the valleys and hills; a land of wheat and barley, vines, and fig trees, pomegranates, olive oil and honey; a land where bread will not be scarce, and you will lack nothing; a land where the rocks are iron, and you can dig copper out of the hills. When you have eaten and are satisfied praise the lord your GOD for the good land, HE has given you".

"And praise the lord your GOD for the good land HE has given you. Eva did. Eva praised her God and preached and lived the glory of GOD.

Eva and the Honolka family departed Europe from Bremerhaven Germany aboard the USS General Harry Taylor. We spent two weeks on the ocean sailing through the English Channel, to the South American city of Puerto of Cabello, where my sister Vlasta remembers people throwing bananas to the refugees on board the Taylor. We arrived at the Demarcation port of New Orleans in May of 1951; Eva was 14 years old. We arrived as refugees and boarded a train to Cresco, Iowa where our American sponsor Mr. John Kostohryz took us to our first home in America in Protivin, Iowa. We came with the clothes on our backs and three wooden boxes, but we had our freedom. Eva Honolka preached the importance of freedom. She was always grateful to the nation that adopted us, the United States. Eva was patriotic and preached Freedom. To quote "We arrived there hungry, torn, scarred and scared, but there was the promise of opportunity to follow happiness with hope".

From Protivin the family moved to Cedar Rapids, Iowa where my sister Vlasta shares this memory of Eva.

"We had to walk from our home on Hamilton street to our school St. Wenceslaus. The walk was approximately 45 minutes to an hour. Eva had two jobs after school. One was across the street from school, where Eva baby sat 3 children, and when done would walk an hour and a half to Noxera's bakery to clean the bakery after the bakery closed. She would then walk an hour and half home. Her payment was an hourly wage and, an occasional bag of baked goods. Eva kept a small amount of the wages but gave most to mom and dad to help support the family." Eva preached the importance of love of family, of being of service, of giving of yourself.

From Cedar Rapids Iowa, in 1955 the family moved to the Amana Colonies of Iowa where Eva's father John Honolka became the general manager of the Amana Bakery. This is a story unto itself but suffice it to say that all the children worked at the Amana Bakery. All of us were expected to work and go to school. We did both. That was what was expected. We worked hard. Eva Honolka preached the dignity of work, the importance of hard work. Eva worked hard all her life.

The love of Eva Honolka's life was LTC Frank Charles Newman. Born in Nepomuk, Czechoslovakia, Frank himself fled Czechoslovakia and was a refugee of communism. Frank enlisted in the U.S Army in Germany. He worked himself through the ranks, from a private (E1) to become a highly decorated, master aviator and commissioned "mustang" officer of the 101st aviation company. Franks journey is a story unto itself. The marriage was an arranged marriage. At 19 years old Eva flew by herself to Texas and was married 7th of July 1956. She was married in the dress she bought herself. Eva Honolka Newman personally told me the gentlemen that Frank Charles Newman was. After the marriage he took her home, showed her the bedroom, and stated this is where you will sleep, I will sleep on the couch until you learn to love me. Wow. Frank Charles Newman was an awesome man.

I was a small boy at the funeral in Marengo, Iowa of Eva, and Frank's first-born son Michael Frank Newman in April of 1957. Eva was now 20 years old.

"Do you not know, can you not see, that from dust you were made and to dust you shall return, but my soul and spirit will rise again." This is what almighty GOD revealed to Eva. Through this loss Eva's deep faith in almighty GOD and HIS kingdom began to be revealed to be shaped. Eva Honolka Newman was a strong woman of faith. Eva preached the importance of faith. Eva lived her faith. Eva's faith sustained her. Eva's faith carried her through the death of her beloved Frank Charles Newman, Frank being killed in Viet Nam, February 24, 1970. To quote "I became a widow, with three little children, two boys and a girl, and when the time came, I pinned Frank's wings on my sons chest, and I was proud to be the wife of a soldier who gave his all". Yes, Eva was patriotic and preached patriotism and freedom. Eva's faith carried her through the death of her son Steven Alan, the death of her son John Zeke, the death of her son Sidney Homer, the death of her father. Upon the death of her mother in 1987 Eva was 50 years old. Eva preached to appreciate life as it is given to us by a power beyond ourselves. Eva was a strong woman of faith and lived her faith.

Eva's final journey started in Montgomery, Alabama. For thirty-three years she was employed by the state of Alabama as a receptionist and tour guide at the state capital and first white house of the confederacy. Her final journey home carried her from her beloved home at 9 Calhoun road here in Montgomery, Alabama. The only place she had in her life to put down roots. Her GOD carried her to Birmingham Alabama to the assisted living facility at the Oaks Parkwood where Eva sustained a debilitating stroke. You cannot script life. The whys of life are stated in the scriptures, "My ways are not your ways declares the lord thy GOD". "A man thinketh in his heart the way he should go, but it is GOD that directs our steps". I strongly believe that after the journey that this proud, strong, courageous, woman of faith took she needed a rest. GOD knew that Eva would never slow down or stop. GOD had to intervene. At the full ripening of her soul, she was taken home, "where GOD wiped away the tears from her eye's. She is now free and is home with the ones GOD blessed her with.

True freedom lies in the arms of GOD. The belief in, understanding of, looking to, trusting in, walking with, and having a personal relationship with the great Alpha and Omega, the beginning, and the end.

John 1:5 NIV

"In the beginning was the word, and the word was with GOD, and the word was GOD. He was with GOD in the beginning. Through HIM all things were made that been made. In HIM was life and that life was the light of men." Eva was a bright light. She was a beacon.

The freedoms of this country have been bought with a price. Freedom is not free. Millions of brave people have sacrificed, many paying the ultimate price to defend that freedom.

Eva Honolka Newman was a product of war, of escape from communism, of brokenness, of loss, of sacrifice, of resiliency, of courage and hard work. Nothing was given to Eva. She paid the price for everything. She was a human doing always doing. Mostly for others. She loved her GOD; she loved her family, and She loved her countries. She was a gracious host. She loved gardening, loved being in nature, loved going for walks, loved to read, loved to sing, she played the piano, the harmonic, the accordion. She could sew. Was an excellent cook. She decorated cakes, was athletically inclined in gymnastics and snow skiing. She was multitalented. She was not stingy; she was overly generous with everything that GOD blessed her with.

"it is more blessed to give than to receive" and Eva did.

Who was Eva? What was Eva? Why was Eva the way she was? What influenced Eva's life? How was Eva molded and shaped? To understand Eva Honolka Newman, one needs to understand her journey. Yet what I have shared is but a small part of that journey. How often did Eva sacrifice herself for the betterment of someone else? How many beautiful awards were presented to Eva, including the prestigious (DAR) award, Daughters of the American revolution, of which in its 104-year history only 8 medals have been awarded to "outstanding naturalized American citizens." How many hundreds of inspirational speeches did she present including, at the invitation of the Czech government, being the guest speaker and guest of honor at commemoration ceremonies at the aviation museum in Prague in April 1995, helping to commemorate the end of world war two in Europe. How many hundreds of patriotic speeches did she present? How many dignitaries paid her homage? How many volunteer efforts were given by Eva including sponsorships of international officers stationed at Maxwell Air Force base, girls state, boys state and the Hugh Obrien foundation. How much loss did she endure? What did Eva share with you? How did Eva help you? Is your life better today because of Eva Honolka Newman?

Proverbs 31:29-31 NIV

"Many women do noble things, but you surpass them all. Charm is deceptive, and beauty is fleeting; but a woman who fears the lord is to be praised. Give her the reward she has earned, and let her works bring her praise at the city gate.

Thank you.

2020 Guest Book Memories for
Eva Honolka Newman

in August of 2002 at her home in Montgomery, AL. The moment I saw her it felt like I had known her for ages .... such a beautiful soul. For those 18 or so years I knew Eva, she was like a second mother to me ... always giving never asking for anything in return. Will always be in our hearts and memories. Rest in peace angel! Arben, Kate, Lea and Bora.

Arben Skivjani, Friend

I met Eva in Montgomery back in 2004 or 2003. My friend came to town for visit so I showed him around downtown and we walked by FWHOC where she worked. The place looked closed, so we walked past it. And then it was like something stopped me, so I looked over my shoulder and then walked back to the front door and opened it. My friend walked back to. So we looked around, speaking in Czech language saying silly things and then there she was in her little gift shop. Just listening to us. Would not say a thing until we were about to leave. And she shocked us with talking to us in Czech language as well. Let me know if you have any questions boys. She invited us home later for cup of tea and we apologized for some of the things we said about her museum. Well I will never forget the feeling inside when I walked back to her museum. Destiny's call for sure. She was like a Mother to me.
Patrik Ricica, Friend

Aunt Eva's life was a blessing to all, and a memory to treasure. She had the most beautiful blue eyes that sparkled, and a smile and laugh that was contagious. Her hugs made you feel so warm and loved. She had a gift of lifting everyone up around her. I learned a lot about the history of our family through her amazing stories and will always be grateful for that. I admired her for being able to overcome all the many obstacles and tragedies in her life, and still see the good in everyone and everything. She was always positive. I also admired her love for her family and for her country! She was a strong, courageous, and beautiful person inside and out that will truly be missed by all. Love always, Susie (Niece), Derek, Gabby, and Lexi Missimo

September 3, 1989 was the first time Don took me to meet his sister Eva, and her special man Arvis. We met in Vicksburg, Ms. and toured the Vicksburg National Military Park. I was amazing by a little woman that knew so much about history and spoke with a cute Czech accent. Eva loved people, adored her family, and had many wonderful friends. She valued time spent with them, always a gracious listener and encourager. Eva focused on others with a servant's heart. She became a sister. I cherish every card, letter, or book she sent me, full of her writings. I made her a promise in May of 2019 to write and publish her story reflecting on the Honolka history with an in-depth detail of her life. The book will be published in 2021. The book title is "SILENCED". Now my dear sweet Eva you may rest in peace. I love you and will always remember and pass on the lessons I learned from you. Sharon Honolka, Sister-in-Law

She was a beautiful bouquet of flower beautifying and cheering the surroundings in her own gentle generous way no matter where she went and asking nothing in return.

Patricia, Sister

My Aunt Eva was special. She was fun, sweet, loving and always the life of the parties. Her presence was contagious and always made everyone smile. She saw the good in people and I will miss her. I will never forget in 2001 at the family reunion in Alabama Eva was a little stressed one day. She asked me if I wanted to see Montgomery history with her and of course I thought that would be cool. We started and then ended up at a brewery. Lol. She told me that she needed that time away and thanked me for hanging out with her. We had a blast. My oldest son Carson still sleeps with a little stuffed rabbit Eva mailed us when he was born 10 years ago. Every night he goes to bed the memory will always remain. RIP ♡ Danny Honolka, Nephew

Eva was a great friend to my spouse Philip Carroll Callahan and to me. We loved her because she was a very precious friend. Her door was always open as was ours. Whenever we needed her, she was there and likewise whenever she needed anything, we would always chip in to help. I was sorry to see her go away from Montgomery but was incredibly happy to see her a couple of times after she had moved to Birmingham. She even spent the night once when she wanted to be with her friend who was getting a divorce. Eva was a true friend to everyone!

Nesta M. Callahan, Friend

To know Eva was to love her. She always made everyone she met feel so special. Words cannot describe how much she will be missed by her sister and brothers. John and Sandy Honolka, Brother, and Sister-in-Law

Eva was remarkably close to her three brothers Don, John and Tom and sister. Spoke with Patricia least once a day. Eva was glad to hook up with Cousin Hans, later in life.

Sharon Honolka, Sister-in-law

I am so sorry to learn of Eva's passing. She was a dear friend, "sister," and neighbor to my mom, Sara Moseley. She was a wonderful lady who shared her stories and love of this country with all who asked. Kay Keeshan, Friend

Grandma I love you and I miss you. There are no perfect words to sum up your time on this earth, but I know if anyone knew the right words to say, it was you. You were such a beautifully gifted speaker. You had such a passion for this country and for your family. I could count on you to be wearing your red, white, and blue. You were thankful for what this country gave you and I am forever grateful for what you gave to our lives. You passed on your love for cats and even got me a cat of my own. I will forever remember you through every elephant ear and American flag I see. I rest knowing you have made it to your true home.

You always told me, "this isn't goodbye, but until we meet again". Kelly Slaten, Granddaughter

My best friend. I will always love you. You deserved so much more than how the last two years of your life went. My heart is shattered but I know now you are fully restored. I could go on, but that is between us. Rest peacefully, my hero, our matriarch. Melanie Lynne Newman, Granddaughter

2020 Obituary of John Honolka, Jr.

John Honolka, Jr., 74, passed away peacefully surrounded in love by his family on November 22, 2020. He was born in Trutnov, Czechoslovakia on June 8, 1946.

In pursuit of Freedom and Liberty, John and his family came to America in 1951 as refugees from Czechoslovakia. John graduated from Amana High School, in Amana, Iowa. He joined the Navy in June 1965, and he was honorably discharged in May of 1967 where he received a National Defense Service Medal. He was married to Sandra Cooper Honolka, devoted wife of 51 years, on September 6, 1969.

John had a successful forty-year career in the automobile industry in sales and sales management. When he was in sales, he was also known as "J.J." as customers had a hard time remembering his last name.

He had a passion for classic cars, gardening, camping, fishing, barbecuing, and watching his beloved children and grandchildren play soccer. He was preceded in death by his parents, John and Jarmila Honolka; sister, Eva Honolka Newman, and nephews, Cody Honolka, Jon Jeffrey Honolka, Michael Newman, Steve Newman, John Walker, and Sidney Walker.

He will be greatly missed by his wife, Sandra Cooper Honolka; his daughter, Susan Missimo and husband, Derek; his son, Danny Honolka and wife, Carrie, and his beautiful grandchildren, Gabriella Missimo, Alexis Missimo, Carson Honolka, and Cayden Honolka. He leaves behind his sister, Pat Shaver; his brothers, Don Honolka and wife, Sharon, and Tom Honolka and wife, Leslie.

John was a devoted husband, Dad, and "Papa" with a giving heart. Life with John was never dull, He loved to have parties by the pool while he was barbecuing ribs and brisket. With a twinkle in his eyes, his rosy red cheeks, and his authentic white beard, he loved to be Santa at Christmas. He attended many parties, schools, and children hospitals as Santa. He also had great love and compassion for animals.

Funeral services will be 10:00am, Monday, December 7, 2020 at JE Foust and Son Funeral Home in Grapevine, TX.

Burial with Navy honors will follow at the Dallas Fort Worth National Cemetery.

2020 Eulogy for John Honolka, Jr.

June 8, 1946 – November 22, 2020
Given by his youngest brother, Tomas Honolka

December 7, 2020
JE Foust and Son Funeral Home
523 South Main Street
Grapevine, TX 76051

Hebrews 2:10-13 NIV

In bringing many sons to glory, it was fitting that GOD, for whom and through whom everything exists, should make the author of their salvation perfect through suffering. Both the one who makes men holy and those who are made holy are of the same family. So, Jesus is not ashamed to call them brothers. HE says, "I will declare your name to my brothers; in the presence of the congregation, I will sing your praises. I will put my trust in HIM. Here I am, and the children GOD has given me".

My brother John suffered and has passed and is in glory. Christ suffered and died to pay a debt we could not pay and lives. Christ is not ashamed to welcome John into HIS family. Christ is not ashamed to call John a brother. In the presence of the ones gone on before John, Christ sings John's praises. We can all trust in Christ. HE has saved the children GOD has given HIM.

I have been asked to speak of my brother John. It is impossible proposition to speak of a life of 74 years. I have prayed for the essence of my brother John to be revealed and the glory of the GOD that we serve. You cannot script life. Proverbs 16:9 speaks "in his heart a man plans his course, but it is GOD that determines his steps".

I want to thank everyone in attendance here today for your love and support of my brother John and his family, his wife Sandra, and children Susie and Danny. I will acknowledge our most honored guest here today our lord and savior Jesus Christ. John was a wonderful brother, husband, father, and friend. Psalm 34:18 tells us "the lord is close to the broken hearted and saves those who are crushed in the spirit." Know that GOD is close, that HE understands, and that HE will heal your broken heart and renew your spirit. John is home. John's journey is over, his work is done. GOD has wiped away his tears. John has been delivered from his suffering. He has been set free. All of us will see John again in that glorious place GOD has provided.

Who was John? What was John? Why was John the way he was? Each of us here has a place in Johns story. Each of us here can answer the who, what and why of John. Most especially his wife of 51 years, his children, 4 grandchildren, brothers, and sister. I will do my best to tell Johns story.

My brother John was born June 8, 1946 in Trutnov, Czechoslovakia. He was the 4th of 5 children of our father John Honolka and mother Jarmila Kralik Honolka, Eva, Vladimir, Vlasta, John and me Tomas. My brother John was born after the close of World War two in May 1945. Our father was born in the Sudeten land where his parents were German's. Despite German origins our father considered himself Czech, as He attended a Czech school. During the German occupation of the Czechoslovakia our father was treated as a Czech, spoke the Czech language and raised his children in the Czech manner.

At the close of world war two eastern Europe along with Czechoslovakia was taken over by the communists. Our father was an independent successful businessman who owned Koruna fancy pastries. Under communism the state owns everything, and our father's business was taken from him and nationalized. He was told that "no man should own so much, or control this many workers, This is permitted only to the state". Our father refused to be indoctrinated into communism and was arrested and jailed for "illegal activities against the government and not cooperating in the best interest of society and the state." Our father was held 3 days in jail and interrogated and deemed politically unreliable. Upon his release from jail on September 16, 1948 our father was sentenced to 6 months forced labor in a coal mine by the district political committee. Fearing further persecution, the family decided to flee the area.

The Honolka family escaped to Hungary, we were captured, arrested, and jailed. Upon release and escape from jails and prisons the family was separated for 9 months. With the aid of the American red cross the family was reunited in the French sector of Austria, the city of Salzburg to be exact. We spent 3 years in the agonizingly slow process of immigrating to America in the displaced person's camp of Regenfeld in Lindau, Germany, where I was born the last of 5 children.

Upon acceptance for immigration to America our family departed Bremerhaven, Germany on the USS Harry Taylor. We sailed through the English channel and spent two weeks on the open sea finally arriving at our demarcation point of New Orleans in May 1951. Our family arrived as displaced persons, poor, broken but free. The family boarded a train to Cresco, Iowa where our American sponsor Mr. John Kostohrys met the family and took us to Protivin, Iowa. That was our first home in America. My brother John was 5 years old.

Our family struggled our first four to five years in America. Our first home had no electricity, no indoor plumbing, we used gas lanterns for light, we walked everywhere, had no car, no money, we were extremely poor. My brothers and sisters carried metal milk buckets to town and back for drinking water. We bathed in a cement drinking trough for cows. Fortunately, GOD blessed us with two families, the Milo Naxera's and the Andrew Polehna's that assisted us in a move to Walford, Iowa then to Cedar Rapids, Iowa. Our conditions started to improve.

For the Honolka family the following scripture applies:

Deuteronomy 8:7-10 NIV

"for the lord, your GOD is bringing you into a good land, a land with streams and pools of water, with springs flowing in the valleys and hills, a land with wheat and barley, vines, and fig trees, pomegranates, olive oil and honey, a land where bread will not be scarce, and you will lack nothing; a land where the rocks are iron, and you can dig copper out of the hills. When you have eaten and are satisfied, praise the lord your GOD for the good land HE has given you."

My brother John praised the lord his GOD by being John. Good hearted, generous, fun loving, mischievous, grateful, giving, loyal and faithful. John praised his GOD in his own way, by being John.

When John was 9 years old our family moved to the Amana Colonies in Iowa. The Amana colonies were settled in the 1800's by German immigrants to America. There are 7 small villages on 25.000 acers of forests, hills, rivers, and ponds. It was a boy's paradise. The Amana's were known for their shops making hand made products, restaurants, and farming. We came to that area of Iowa as our father became the manager of the Amana Society bakery in South Amana, Iowa. He turned a small rural German bakery into a phenomenally successful operation servicing multiple states with German bakery products. All of us were expected to work in the bakery and attend school. That is what was expected. To work and attend school. You did both. All of us were adept at running the mixers, dividers, sheeters, proof boxes, slicers, ovens, flour bins, the mixing of the ingredients, night sponges and bread routes. Our father taught us a hard work ethic. My brother John carried that hard work ethic through his entire life.

As boys John and I spent much of our time in GODS creation. The fields, forests, ponds, and rivers of 25.000 acers of fields, forests, ponds, and rivers. In the winter sled riding, building snow forts, snow men, snow igloos, snowball fights, ice skating. In the summer trudging through the fields and forests, camping out, building fires, fishing, riding our bicycle's. We listened to songs like "The Hot Rod Lincoln", "Mr. Custer" "Sink the Bismarck" and "The Battle of New Orleans". We made forts out of corn stalks in the middle of corn fields. We built huts in the timber out of fallen branches. We swam, fished, and hunted bull frogs at the south Amana pond, We swam and fished in the Iowa river, we rode out bicycles to the West Amana dam and fished for carp, cropie, bull head, catfish, and pike. We hunted rabbits, pheasants, and ground squirrels. We made bombs out of M 80's. We would go into hay barns and capture pigeons and keep them as pets. We had BB guns and shot at most everything including at each other, windows, birds, dogs, cats, cows, targets, and John loved shooting bulls in the nuts. All these activities carried on into Johns teen years. John learned to love the outdoors. The fields, forests, ponds, and rivers. John loved to hunt, camp and fish. You can take the boy out of the country, but you will never take the country out of the boy. The country never left John. He spoke of it until the end. John is home. I rejoice in knowing my brother has been delivered. Free to pursue in GODS eternal kingdom the desires of his heart, no longer tethered to a broken suit of flesh.

John attended Amana high school where John was a multiyear letterman in basketball and baseball. John was a talented athlete. John was also a multiyear letterman in pranks, hijinks, school suspensions, semi reasonable grades, girlfriends, drag racing and in the German colonies of Amana you drank a lot of beer. John drove a 57 Chevrolet convertible with a 265 cubic inch, bored and stroked, high lift cam, dual quad carbs with a 3 speed on the floor. It was the era of the muscle cars and John had one. That love for cars never left John. John was also a multi vehicle lettermen in falling asleep at the wheel of vehicles as several of the Amana bread trucks and one of Johns personal cars can attest to. When he was not crashing a vehicle, he was picked up for speeding. John was a real Dennis to Menace. A prankster to teachers, friends, and foes alike. John loved his fun. Mischievous, fun loving, good hearted and popular.

My brother John was 19 years old when he enlisted and departed for service in the United States Navy. My mother, father and I were at the airport in Cedar Rapids, Iowa when he left in June of 1965. I was sad to see my brother leave. I am deeply sad today. My brother served on the USS Van Voorhis (DE-1028). The Van Voorhis was a destroyer escort based out of Newport Rhode Island. She primarily conducted operations in the Western Atlantic. In August 1966, the USS Van Voorhis rendezvoused with the destroyer escort "USS Hammerberg", guided missile frigate "USS Leahy", and submarine "USS Requin" off Trindad to participate in operation "Unitas VII" through November. In 1966 and 1967, the warship made cruises around South America in which she visited several south American ports and participated in bilateral and multi-lateral exercises with warships of various south American countries. I remember my brother speaking of the hazing initiation the tad pools received when they crossed the equator and the numerous ports they docked at. The term "drunken sailor" was not invented by my brother, but he lived the tradition, as proof was the rather large tattoos on each of John's forearm's. My brother was 21 years old when he was honorably discharged in May 1967 and spent two more years in the Naval reserve. He returned to the Amana colonies and bought him another muscle car. A blue 1969 Chevelle super sport, 396 cubic inch, 4 speed. John once again showed his lettermen ability for falling asleep at the wheel and destroying cars. Every time John crawled into a car, I can imagine GOD sending an angel and saying, "anchors aweigh boys here he comes".

When John was 22 years old our father's prosperous bakery operations sent John to Texas to deliver bread in the Dallas Fort Worth area. In June of 1968 John met the love of his life Sandra Cooper. They met at an "American Graffiti" type drive in hamburger stand on Park Row in Arlington, Texas called Powell's Hamburgers. John got Sandra's phone number that night and though not expecting to get a call from John Sandra did. Sandra tells me John took her to many special restaurants, had many laughs and good times, went many different places and on September 6, 1969 they were married. The honeymoon was in Acapulco, Mexico. They had a private suite with its own pool and a jeep to explore the country.

John spent 40 successful years in the automobile industry. The automobile industry demands long hours with lots of nights, weekends, and straight commission stress. John built a loyal customer base, sold many automobiles, and spent many years as the sales manager of various automobile agencies. John spent long hours in that industry, worked his ass off and was successful.

John and Sandra were married for 51 years, have two children Susie and Danny and four grandchildren. 51 years brings many challenges, trials, tribulations, tears, and laughter. I want to publicly thank you Sandra for your loving loyalty to my brother and accepting, loving, and taking care of him. Life is not an easy task. Though imperfect and broken John was a loyal brother, husband, and father. He would give you the shirt off his back. He was very giving and generous.

So how do we conclude this eulogy?

I ask for your forgiveness for not mentioning the special memories you and I all have of John. They will remain forever with us and perhaps we can share the memories together.

From Danny Honolka, John's son, I will read the words to the song by "Pearl Jam",

"Man of the Hour".
Tidal waves don't beg forgiveness
Crashed and on their way
Father he enjoyed collisions; others walked away
A snowflake falls in May

And the doors are open now
As the bells are ringing out
'Cause the man of the hour
Is taking his final bow
Goodbye for now

Nature has its own religion
Gospel from the land
Father ruled by long division
Young men they pretend
Old men comprehend

And the sky breaks at dawn
Shedding light upon this town
They'll all come around
'Cause the man of the hour
Is taking his final bow
Goodbye for now

And the road
The old man paved
The broken seams along the way
The rusted signs, left just for me
He was guiding me, love, his own way

Now the man of the hour is taking his final bow
As the curtain comes down
I feel that this is just goodbye for now

From Susie Missimo, John's daughter. Her post appeared on her Face book page.

November 24 at 9:01 AM

I have had a hard time coming to terms with the reality of doing this post. I lost my first true love and hero, my father on Sunday evening. I have not even been able to find words, I am just heartbroken. My Dad was a special man. Since I was a little girl, he encouraged me to participate in sports, particularly soccer and track. Not only did he encourage, but he also told me you can beat the boys. Such powerful words to tell a little girl, and I did beat the boys, and he would belly laugh. At the time I did not recognize what a gift to me that was, but the sense of confidence those words instilled in me I will always cherish and carry with me to this day.

My Dad made me feel strong and beautiful. He has done the same for his Granddaughters as well. He was always cheering them on at almost every single soccer game they played in - rain, shine, hot, or cold in Texas weather. He has always been there for his family in good times and bad. He was our rock. He had a heart of gold. During the Holidays he would visit schools or hospitals dressed as Santa to cheer kids up.

He brought people together with his parties and famous ribs. He was the boss of all the best pit bosses. He could make a mean rib that would fall off the bone and melt in your mouth.

He loved the outdoors- hunting, fishing, gardening. My love of gardening to this day is because of him. Dad, you provided, protected, sacrificed for us and your Country as a Navy Veteran, and gave your love to us endlessly. To me you were the perfect role model, and I will always love and adore you. It is your turn for peace and fun in Heaven. You can do all the hunting and fishing you want now. You will be missed dearly here, but I will see you soon to join you in the festivities!

And I will conclude with the following lyrics.

From John's brothers and sister, the words to the "The Hollies" song,

"He Aint heavy, He's My Brother".
The road is long
With many a winding turn
That leads us to who knows where
Who knows where
But I'm strong
Strong enough to carry him
He ain't heavy, he's my brother

So on we go
His welfare is of my concern
No burden is he to bear
We'll get there

For I know
He would not encumber me
He ain't heavy, he's my brother

If I'm laden at all
I'm laden with sadness
That everyone's heart
Isn't filled with the gladness
Of love for one another

It's a long, long road
From which there is no return
While we're on the way to there
Why not share

And the load
Doesn't weigh me down at all
He ain't heavy he's my brother

He's my brother
He ain't heavy, he's my brother, he ain't heavy

2020 Guest Book Memories for John Honolka, Jr.

John, I know you were watching from above. Most likely surrounded by your Mother, Father, Sister, Mother-in-law, Father-in-law, and Nephew. Everyone doing the happy dance to have you in their presence.

The smile and twinkle in your bright blue eyes as you watched your "Homecoming", Celebration of Life" or "Memorial Service". easily imagined. Sandy carefully considered every decision so it would be special for you. And it was.

You where more than a brother and brother-in-law. You were a friend that will be missed beyond words. Never to be forgotten will be our foursome vacations and Sunday dinners.

Don and I will not 'get over' you moving to the other side. We will learn to live with it. We will heal and we will rebuild ourselves around the loss we have suffered. We will be whole again, but never the same. Until we meet again, Don and Sharon Honolka

I am so sorry about the loss of sweet John. He was a lovely friend and neighbor and I know he was loved by many. We will keep him forever in our hearts. Holly Hitt Niner

John made our family a part of his when we met over 12 years ago. He welcomed us into the crazy soccer world that he loved and always had a smile and a great joke/story to share. I will miss the bear hugs; belly laughs and beautiful blue eyes! I will miss him "fighting" I had the pleasure of being his Elf on one of his Santa ventures! John, your heart left a huge mark on this planet! Keep an eye on us. Love you, Liz Andrews.

I will never forget Papa taking Lexi and I fishing, taking us to Braum's, making us "French toast", his sparkly blue eyes, rosy cheeks, his warm "Santa" hugs, seeing him smile and cheer us on at every single soccer game, and more. Papa was a friend to anyone who had a conversation with him. He loved animals, riding Harley Davidsons, and makings ribs that would drop off the bone. Papa, I miss you every day, and many little things remind me of you everywhere lately. I feel you close to me when I see anything beautiful in nature or an American flag blowing in the wind. Rest In Peace Papa, I will see you again one day in Heaven. Granddaughter, Gabriella Missimo

Eva's Noted Scriptures

Psalm 119:105

Thy word is a lamp unto my feet, and a light unto my path. King James Version

> Your word is a lamp to guide me and a light for my path. Good News English Version

Jeremiah 29:11

For I know the "thoughts that I think toward you, saith the LORD, thoughts of peace, and not of evil, to give you an expected end. King James Version

> I alone know the plans I have for you, plans to bring you prosperity and not disaster, plans to bring about the future you hope for. Good News English Version

Psalm 71:19

Now also when I am old and grey-headed, O God, forsake me not; until I have shewed thy strength unto this generation, and the power to everyone that is to come. King James Version

> Now that I am old and my hair is gray, do not abandon me, O God. Be with me while I proclaim your power and might to all generations to come. Good News English Versions

Galatians 6: 7-8

Do not deceived; God is not mocked: for "whatsoever a man soweth, that shall he also reap. For he, that soweth to his flesh shall of the flesh reap corruption: but he that soweth to the Spirit shall of the Spirit reap life everlasting. King James Version

Do not deceive yourselves; no one makes a fool of God. A person will reap exactly what he plants. If he plants in the field of his natural desires, from it he will gather the harvest of death; if he plants in the field of the Spirit, from the Spirit he will gather the harvest of eternal life. Good News English Versions

One Big Circle

Words written by Eva Honolka Newman – Date Unknown

I am little intimidated to recount events that so much has been written about. An era of the 20th Century, the 2nd World War and take over by communism.

Suffering, pain, loss of human dignity and an over blown human ego of Hitlers power and might.

If man has the desire to war – we as humans have not come out of the mind set of cave man to "Hunt and Kill". Therefore, the suffering of humans continues. There are small minutes of beauty and peace. The human heart's longing for the infinite – the spiritual touch to enter each human soul to achieve its greatness.

Man is like a meadow of beautiful flowers. We cannot change the daisy into a rose, yet each has a beauty of its own to be admired and respected for its uniqueness that contributes to the whole earth.

Our earth was created as one big circle, and everybody is included. We the people of this earth have invented many small circles, and, in that mindset, we are directing each circle believing theirs is the way to heaven. If you do not go according to their laws, you are excluded.

If such took place in the universe it would be total chaos.

This was the end of Eva's writing.

When I originally typed "One Big Circle", I asked myself "What is Eva talking about?" "What is she attempting to tell us".

I asked Tom, Patricia, and Don to read "One Big Circle". Tom said: "My take would be man is a fallen creature and those who fail to remember history are doomed to repeat it. As a people United, we stand, divided we will fall".

It is now February 2021; the past year has been consumed by the Covid-19 pandemic, the death of George Floyd, the national (indeed global) uprising against anti-Black racism, rioting in the streets, looting stores as a form of retribution, burning down Federal buildings, tearing down of historical statues, burning of the American Flag, a hateful Presidential election, everyone is fighting, people are killing each other for no apparent reason, lawmakers vowing to disband police department, impeachment of a President for the 2nd time, and the stock market is on a roller coaster. I am glad Eva is watching from above and I know she is shaking her head. What is happening to her beloved United States of America?

I will leave "One Big Circle" the way it was written by Eva. What do you think Eva was attempting to tell us? I look forward to your response at sharonhonolka@gmail.com.

God Bless You and Yours, Sharon

YouTube Video

Sharing The Heart of Europe
Maxwell Gunter Air Force
February 5, 2016

You.tube.com/watch?v=LOcYWZKXC-w

Printed in the United States
by Baker & Taylor Publisher Services